Creating Fat Content

Boost Website Traffic with Visitor-Grabbing, Google-Loving Web Content

By Dr. Andy Williams

http://webcontentstudio.com

http://ezseonews.com

Contents

What people are saying about this book

"Forget all the mumbo jumbo about how to outwit Google in the Search Engine ranking game with all those fancy tools etc.. You might just possibly get away with some trickery and "thin" sites for a little while, but the big G will catch up with you... probably sooner rather than later.

Get this book instead, read it and more importantly act on the solid (and long-term) sound advice it dishes out in spades." **Harry**

"Excellent book that is bang up to date when it comes to creating content that might actually get you ranking in the search engines. This is not theory but actual research that has led to the creation of this book." **David Sharp**

"I always look forward to anything from Andy and this hasn't disappointed." **Trevor Greenfield**

"Creating Web Content is the first easy to read explanation I've found that shows me how to create great content pleasing both the search engines and my audience as well." **Chris Cobb**

"Well written and easy to understand. I have never been disappointed with any of the Internet info books I have bought from Dr. Andy Williams!" **J. Tanner**

"I have been buying Andy's products for a long time. I was hoping he would write this book. I am ranking on the top pages of Google for a lot of my content. I think this book is the best one he has wrote." **Bill Roberts**

Introduction - A short history of search

When we think of search engines, most of us immediately think of Google. However, when I started working online, Google did not exist. We had other search engines though, and lots of them. Here are the main ones I remember:

1. Infoseek (1995 - 2001)
2. Magellan (1995 - 2001)
3. Lycos (1994 - still going today, though it now depends on All The Web for search results).
4. WebCrawler (1994 - still going today, though it gets search results from other engines).
5. Yahoo (1994 - Still going today).
6. Excite (1995 - still going today, though Dogpile now provides its search results).
7. Altavista (1995 - bought by Yahoo in 2003).
8. HotBot (1996 - bought by Lycos in 1998). This one was re-launched in July 2011 using a robot for its mascot.

If you have been online for any length of time, I am sure a few of those will ring a bell. Some, like Yahoo are still going today, and of course we also have Bing as one of the top 3. However, there really has only been one winner in the search engine wars - Google.

If you could go back a few years and check out the Google search results, you'd see a very different set of search results (often called SERPs which stands for search engine results pages) to the ones we see today. In fact, even going back one year would probably show that Google has been through massive changes in the way it ranks content.

However, there is one thing that hasn't changed much with search engines like Google. They have always wanted to show the most relevant and high quality results to their users.

In the early days of online search, the engines would typically try to match the words a user typed into the search box, with the words on the web pages in their database.

For example, if someone typed in "Up Periscope game", then the search engine would go through the documents in the database looking for any page that contained the phrase "up periscope game". If it found one, then it could return this match to the searcher, and the search engine was happy. The search engine would be even happier if it could find several documents with that exact phrase, giving the searcher

1

more results, more choice and ultimately keeping them happy so they would return next time they wanted to find information.

This is where the problems began. If there were several documents, each containing the phrase "up periscope game", which one does the search engine put first? Second? And so on.

To me, the obvious answer is to put the best one first, and then order the rest according to quality. This way the searcher would have more chance of finding a page that meets their needs quickly by clicking on the top result.

But how does a search engine determine quality?

Today, that is a closely guarded secret involving hundreds of different factors, but it wasn't always that way.

In the late 90s, there were relatively few web pages out there, and search engines just seemed happy if they could find a match for a search term. Although I am sure things were a little more complicated than that, it appeared that ranking pages was done on the basis that if a page contained a search phrase twice, it was better than a page that only contained the phrase once. Therefore it was easy to rank a group of pages from best to worst. The page that contained the search phrase the most number of times won.

It almost seems unbelievable now, but back in those days, if you wanted to rank for a search phrase, you could look at the page currently in position one, count the number of times it used the search phrase, and then write your own page to contain the phrase one more time. Bingo, an instant number one ranking!

In the late 90s, people building websites would find the phrases they wanted to rank for, and then build a page for each phrase. They would include the phrase on their page just enough times to beat the current number one ranking.

As more and more websites were built, you can imagine the type of results you would see. Keyword stuffed nonsense that ranked simply because the phrase you searched for was found a lot of times on the web page. Clearly something needed to change if search engines were going to evolve into a useful tool.

In 1998, a new kid arrived on the block:

Google!

Larry Page and Sergey Brin were two Ph.D. students and Google was their research project which began in 1996. The first version (as shown above) was hosted on a sub-domain of Stanford University.

As you can see, it started off with 25 million pages. By 2008, Google reported that their index had grown to 1 trillion pages, and then 5 years later, it stood at 30 trillion pages!

Larry and Sergey wanted to find a better way to index and rank documents. Counting the number of times a phrase was found on a page was crude and clearly didn't work. Search engine results were getting filled up with rubbish, written by webmasters trying to force their content to the top.

They introduced Page Rank. I am sure you have heard of it.

Page Rank has been the focus of webmasters ever since Google released details of this new technology. Even today, Page Rank is important, though Google are trying to play down its significance, and today, Page Rank is just one of hundreds of ranking factors.

The idea behind Page Rank was probably a natural one coming from their academic environment. The basic idea was that the more important the web page, the more it would be cited by its peers.

Imagine someone searching Google for "crohn's disease medication". If Google had 10,000 documents that matched that search phrase, instead of showing the one that

3

used the phrase the most times in the top slot, they reasoned that the most important one would be the one that that the most links pointing to it from other web pages.

Page Rank was a kind of citation score for a web page. The more a page was linked to from other documents, the higher the score and the better it would rank for relevant search phrases.

OK, so Page Rank became one of the most important factors in the ranking of a web page, and the more links the better. However, there was still a problem that needed to be addressed.

A web page should only rank for relevant search phrases, irrespective of its Page Rank. If someone searches for "Linux operating system", there is no point showing them a page on CNN about "cat litter", simply because the cat litter page has a high Page Rank.

The sequence of events when someone searches for a phrase is therefore as follows:

1. Searcher types in a phrase.
2. Google finds all pages relevant to that phrase.
3. Google ranks the relevant pages according to Page Rank.

OK, so Page Rank was a major step forward in the ranking of pages, but Google still needed to decide which pages were the most relevant to any particular search term.

In the early days, relevance was determined to a large extent by the words on the page. A page would be determined as relevant if the search term was found on the page. Sound familiar?

In fact, the similarity doesn't stop there.

Given two pages with identical Page Rank, the page that included the search term the most times would often rank the higher of the two.

However, Google were on the lookout for unnatural looking pages. It's not natural for a web page to mention the exact same phrase 50 times in a 500 word article, is it? That would be a density of 10% for that phrase.

But what was a natural looking keyword density? Google needed to determine this, and stop any pages that lay outside of this "natural" density from ranking well.

And so, keyword density became important for webmasters.

Clearly keyword density was not the sole measure of relevancy. However, keyword density was important enough for software to appear that could analyze the top ranking pages on any topic, and tell you exactly what keyword densities those pages were using. By matching those keyword densities, your page would have an advantage over any other page in the niche with the same Page Rank. Keyword densities gave you a competitive advantage!

As the search engines matured, the rules for keyword densities changed.

Instead of simply needing a keyword density of let's say 5% in the document, the webpage needed to include that keyword phrase in a number of different elements on the web page. For example, it helped if the keyword was found in the page filename, meta keywords tag, meta description, the main page headline, the opening paragraph, several other times on the page, in ALT tags and hyperlinks, and so on.

Optimizing a web page became an exercise in trying to stuff the keyword phrase into as many HTML elements on the page as possible.

Webmasters quickly found that there was one particular place a keyword would really help you rank – the domain name.

Enter the era of exact match domains.

A search term like "buy prescription drugs online" would be really competitive and difficult to rank for, requiring a lot of Page Rank (built through inbound links). However, with this exact match loophole in Google, anyone owning a domain that contained that exact phrase would be at a huge advantage, and quickly rise to the top of the search rankings.

Exact Match Domains (EMDs) became more and more visible at the top of the Google SERPs, and many of them were spammy sites with poor content, that didn't deserve to rank for those phrases.

Things like:

Buyprescriptiondrugsonline.com

.. as well as the same domain name using every type of available TLD (Top Level Domain):

- Buyprescriptiondrugsonline.org
- Buyprescriptiondrugsonline.net
- Buyprescriptiondrugsonline.info

- Buyprescriptiondrugsonline.co.uk

This type of exact match domain was found in most sets of search results. They became a quick way to rank for just about anything, and a whole industry of buying and selling EMDs arose.

The reason this loophole existed was because the search engines, Google included, looked at the words on the page to help determine relevance to a search term. In fact, to be more specific, it was the appearance of the **exact search term** on the page that determined relevance. This was something that Google identified as a potential problem very early on. What Google wanted was a more natural way of determining what a page was about.

For example, if someone searched for "cure type 2 diabetes", Google didn't just want to return the pages that included that exact keyword phrase. They wanted to return pages that really were about "curing type 2 diabetes". Those that had the exact phrase and those that were actually about the topic were often not the same thing. That was because of the way webmasters forced their pages to the top using the latest and greatest Google loopholes, even if those pages did not deserve to be at the top based on merit.

What Google were trying to develop was a way to categorize a page based on all of the words and phrases on that page. Using the example above, a good quality page that should rank for the phrase "cure type 2 diabetes" would have words and phrases like this on the page:

type 2 diabetes, blood sugar level, diet and exercise, high blood sugar, type of diabetes, blood glucose, low carb, sugar levels, weight loss, lifestyle changes, diabetes, eat, blood, diet, insulin, sugar, health, weight, glucose, diabetic, eating, control, food, organ, normal, doctor, healthy, carbohydrate, organs, symptom, disease, manage, condition, medication, medicine, research, exercise, resistance, tolerance, lifestyle, treatment, symptoms, remission, pancreas, type, level, high, low, carb, levels, loss.

Why?

Because an authority on the topic would naturally use most of those words to describe how type 2 diabetes could be cured.

Most of those words are ESSENTIAL to explain how type 2 diabetes can be cured, so it follows that any page that does not use them, cannot be an authority on the subject.

The problem for Google was that the type and amount of language analysis required to correctly identify relevant (and quality) content based on related words on a page was just too time consuming for the technology of the day.

However, this type of theme analysis wasn't something that only appeared in the last year or two. Google have been working on this for over a decade.

Back in the year 2000, Michael Campbell wrote the first white paper on themes, and then in 2003, Google bought a company called Applied Semantics which they said would help them "Understand the key themes on web pages".

In a press release announcing the acquisition of Applied Semantics, Sergey Brin stated:

"Applied Semantics is a proven innovator in semantic text processing and online advertising."

"This acquisition will enable Google to create new technologies that make online advertising more useful to users, publishers, and advertisers alike."

The press release went on to say:

> Applied Semantics' products are based on its patented CIRCA technology, which understands, organizes, and extracts knowledge from websites and information repositories in a way that mimics human thought and enables more effective information retrieval. A key application of the CIRCA technology is Applied Semantics' AdSense product that enables web publishers to understand the key themes on web pages to deliver highly relevant and targeted advertisements.

Google had acquired a technology that could help them understand web pages in a similar way to how humans understand something when they are reading it.

Using this new technology, Google went on to release Google Adsense.

Google Adsense, in case you have not heard about it, is a technology that allows Google to show advertisements on relevant web pages. With companies prepared to pay good money to advertise around the web, Google needed to make sure this technology could do more than just find a keyword on a page to confirm relevancy. Google needed to look for keyword "themes" that matched each advertisement.

Applied Semantics was the turning point for Google. It allowed them to accurately determine the theme of a web page so that relevant adverts could be shown on that page. Google took the logical next step – incorporating this technology into the search engine ranking algorithm.

Now, instead of relying on the appearance of the exact search phrase, Google could look for themes appearing on a page to help determine its relevancy to a search term.

Today, having the exact search term on your web page means very little. In fact, I want you to do a little experiment yourself. Go over to Google and search for a three or four word phrase that has some commercial intent (in other words, a phrase someone might type in if they wanted to buy something). This is a good test, because these are the phrases webmasters are trying to rank for.

In the SERPs, Google will highlight the words in your phrase in bold. So, if you searched for "buy prom dress online", Google would highlight the words "buy", "prom", dress" and "online" in the titles and descriptions of the results.

Top 7 **Online** Resources for **Prom Dresses** - about Prom
prom.about.com › ... › Dress Basics › Shopping for Formal Wear ▾
Their **prom dresses** aren't too shabby, either. You can find fabulous options under $70 alongside designer dresses from labels like Nicole Miller and BCBG. **Buy** ...

How many of the top 10 results use the exact search term (buy prom dress online) in their title or description?

I just did the search.

I have Google set up to show me 100 results at a time, so I have the top 100 pages that rank for that term on my screen. By pressing F3 in my Chrome web browser, I can search for the phrase on the page to see how many times the phrase "buy prom dress online" appears in this list of top 100 web page titles and descriptions:

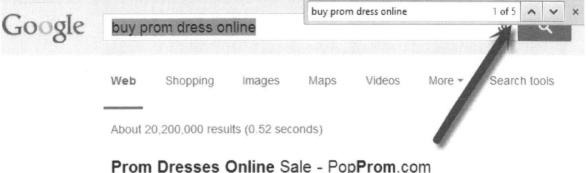

Web   Shopping   Images   Maps   Videos   More ▾   Search tools

About 20,200,000 results (0.52 seconds)

Prom Dresses Online Sale - Pop**Prom**.com
`Ad` www.pop**prom**.com/**Prom-Dresses** ▾
Full Choice,Best Service,75% Off, Taiolr Made,Fast Delivery,**Buy** Now!

    Formal Dresses   Evening Dresses
    Wedding Dresses   Bridesmaid Dresses

Prom dress - Dylanqueen.co.uk
`Ad` www.dylanqueen.co.uk/**PromDresses** ▾
2014 **Prom Dresses**, 2000+ Styles. Tailor Made,From £51, Shop Now!

Buy Prom Dresses - Vogue**PromDresses**.co.uk
`Ad` www.vogue**promdresses**.co.uk/ ▾
All Styles&Color,Up to 75% Off, Custom Made,75% Off Shipping...
Evening Dresses - Bridesmaid Dresses - Quinceanera Dresses - Formal Dresses

Buy Prom Dresses Online - 2014 - Top Prom Websites
www.top**prom**websites.com/**buy-prom-dresses-online**.html ▾
Buy prom dresses online from manually verified authorized retailers.

Buy Wedding Dress **Online**, **Prom Dresses Online** - David's ...
www.davidsbridal.com/Browse_**Buy-Online** ▾   David's Bridal ▾
Shop and **buy** your wedding **dress online** at David's Bridal. Find exclusive offers like
free shipping and daily deals for **online** orders now at David's Bridal!

PromGirl: **Prom Dresses**, Homecoming Dresses, Prom Shoes
www.**prom**girl.com/ ▾
Shop PromGirl for 2014 **prom dresses**, party dresses, prom shoes, designer prom ...
Logo - PromGirl, the **online** super store for **prom dresses**, homecoming party ...
Long Dresses - Shop Prom - Prom Under $200 - Short Dresses

That's 5 times then. In fact, the phrase only appears 3 times in the top 100 titles and descriptions, because one of those occurrences is the actual search phrase I typed it (you can see it highlighted in the screenshot above), and it also appears at the bottom of the page in a section where Google recommends related searches:

9

Searches related to **buy prom dress online**

sell prom dress online	**promgirl homecoming dresses**
buy **wedding** dress online	**should i** buy **a** prom dress online
buy **formal** dress online	buy **blush** prom **dresses** online
buy **dresses** online	buy **used** prom **dresses** online

Whatever YOU search for in this experiment, you are likely to find the exact search phrase in some pages. However, as you can see, it is no longer essential to help a page rank well, and if you use the exact phrase too many times, it is more likely to get your page penalized.

I carried out the above experiment on a few more keyword searches. Here are the results of those:

Term: best compact camera

Number of times the phrase appears on top 100 titles and descriptions: 36

Term: buy nikon d5200

Number of times the phrase appears on top 100 titles and descriptions: 26

Term: best toys for 5 year old boys

Number of times the phrase appears on top 100 titles and descriptions: 5

Term: gift idea for men

Number of times the phrase appears on top 100 titles and descriptions: 1

NOTE: If you do this experiment yourself, don't forget to subtract one for the search term at the top of the results page (which you typed in), and any "Related" search ideas that Google offer at the end of the search results, like this one:

Searches related to **gift idea for men**

birthday gift **ideas** men

gift idea for men **turning 50**

gift idea for men **anniversary**

gift idea for men **who have everything**

gift idea for men **turning 30**

gift idea for men **turning 40**

gift idea for men **40th birthday**

axe hair products gift idea for men

Clearly the old method of optimizing a web page around a keyword phrase no longer works. Therefore, if you are still taking SEO advice from the "keyword phrase & density" gurus, isn't it time you changed your approach to writing content?

Let me show you a better way.

The whole purpose of this book is to give you a plan for writing content that stands a better chance of not only ranking in Google, but staying there.

Before we start looking at how to write content, it's important to know a brief history of the Google algorithm changes. Not only will this help you understand where Google have come from, and where they are headed, but it will reinforce the idea that loopholes get closed, so don't try to beat the system.

A History of Google Updates

As webmasters and content writers, it is important to follow along with what Google are doing, because they never stand still. Webmasters are always trying to find loopholes, and Google is always trying to plug them. In this section, I want to tell you about the major updates Google have gone through, and explain why they were necessary. As I go through these, be aware that I am only telling you about a few major changes that impacted how webmasters optimized their sites. Major updates are given names (I am sure you have heard of Panda and Penguin), much like hurricanes are given names ;) but I'll only tell you the names of the more infamous (from a webmasters point of view) ones.

I should also state here that we don't know with 100% certainty what many of the updates actually did in terms of algorithm changes. What I am listing here is the accepted version of events deduced by webmasters and SEOs around the globe.

Google releases hundreds of updates every year, so it is way beyond the scope of this chapter to even try to list them all. For example, in September 2011, Google CEO Eric Schmidt said that Google has tested over 13,000 possible updates in 2010, and approved 516 of those updates.

One thing Google updates ALL have in common – they are designed to give searchers better results.

Changes in 2003

Webmasters knew that backlinks helped their pages rank, so did everything they could to increase the number of backlinks. In 2003, Google clamped down on webmasters who interlinked their own sites to help ranking. They also came after pages with hidden text (and hidden links).

Also in 2003, the Google Dance was replaced by "Everflux". The Google Dance was something webmasters looked forward to. It was roughly a once a month phenomenon where the index was updated, and as it did, pages jumped around in the rankings for a few days before finally settling at their new position. Everflux by contrast allowed constant updating on a daily basis, meaning ranking could move around at any time during the month, depending on the how well the pages met Google's algorithm.

In September 2003, because of the size of the index (which was expanding rapidly), Google introduces the Supplemental Index. This is where pages that Google felt weren't of a high enough quality were stored. When someone searched at Google, if there were good matches in the main index for the query, they were shown to the searcher. If there were few or no results in the main index, Google could then draw on the supplemental index for results. Webmasters tried very hard to keep their content out of the supplemental index.

Finally in 2003, there was a big change that shook the SEO world. It was called Florida and happened in November 2003, and many websites lost rankings, businesses went bust. This update was designed to eliminate poor quality content that was only ranking because of the SEO techniques employed by the owners. A number of factors would have been taken into account, including pages that stuffed keywords on the page, especially commercially valuable keywords.

Changes in 2004

In 2004, Google's index increased dramatically, meaning they had to work harder to identify the quality.

They looked at inbound link quality, anchor text relevance and probably employed more of their Latent Semantic Indexing (LSI) technology to help them understand synonyms. It also became increasingly important NOT to link to poor quality sites. By linking to poor pages, you were effectively vouching or "voting" for these bad pages. Google warned against this, and referred to it as linking to "bad neighbourhoods". You can see what Google were trying to do here. The threat was clear – link to poor quality and you will be seen as poor quality.

Google were on the lookout for other deceptive SEO tactics, like hidden text and keyword stuffing of meta keyword and description tags.

2004 was also the year of Google's initial public offering (IPO) of shares, raising $1.67 billion.

Changes in 2005

Continuing their attempt to control spammy linking practises, Google (Yahoo & Microsot) introduced the "nofollow" attribute. This allowed webmasters to link to another site without actually vouching for the site. For example, if you wanted to link to a page that might be in a bad neighbourhood, or you thought might become part of a bad neighbourhood in the future, you could add the nofollow attribute to the link, and that would protect you against a Google penalty. This worked because the "nofollow" tag told Google you were not vouching for the site.

A common use for the nofollow tag today is by Wordpress / Blog site owners, who make the comments on their site nofollow. This protects them, because people who leave comments often link to their own websites, and you (as the site owner), do not control those outbound links. By making them nofollow, you are telling Google that you do not vouch for those links.

Algorithmic changes in 2005 probably included duplicate content filters and the way in which URLs with and without the "www." were treated (canonical URLs).

Google also began looking at user search history to personalize search results.

Towards the end of 2005 we saw an update named "Jagger". Jagger was again a quality control measure, targeting low-quality links, like reciprocal links (where websites exchange links with each other) and bought links (where a webmaster pays another webmaster for the link).

Changes in 2006

This was a relatively quite year. In November, Google released an update that changed the way the supplemental index was handled, and how the pages within it were filtered.

Changes in 2007

Google introduced "Universal Search" in May 2007. This was just an integration of news, images, video etc into the search results. It made searching for different types of media a lot more convenient. There was also an update named "Buffy" in June, but Google said that this update was just an accumulation of small changes.

Changes in 2008

In August, Google introduced Google Suggest. This provided suggested search terms in a drop-down box under the main search box.

Changes in 2009

In February we saw "Vince". This update seemed to support the ranking of higher authority "brands". It was all about trust, authority and reputation, and while Google suggested it was a small change, many smaller mom & pop websites suffered.

Changes in 2010

Google "Places" appeared in the search results. This highlighted local businesses in the results, and used the searchers location to provide relevant, local information.

At the end of April/beginning of May, Google introduced a change which impacted long-tail results. Previously, a lot of low quality pages were showing up for long-tail searches (searches with several words), and Google wanted to increase the quality of those results. It did so in the "May Day" update.

In June, we finally saw an update that we had been waiting for, called Caffeine. We had seen a preview of this update in 2009, but it was June 2010 when it was finally rolled out. Caffeine integrated crawling and indexing more closely, resulting in a much fresher index, and a much faster Google.

Google Instant appeared in September, and was a natural evolution of the Google Suggest feature introduced in August 2008.

This is the feature you see today, where Google offers you suggestions as you type your search string. These suggestions are based on previous searches by other users, as Google offers you the most commonly typed phrases that match your incomplete search string.

Google

buffy| 🎤

buffy **the vampire slayer**
buffy **the vampire slayer movie**
buffy **the body**
buffy **wiki**
buffy **the vampire slayer wiki**
buffy **waltrip**
buffy **season 10**
buffy**shot**
buffy **the vampire slayer episodes**
buffy **season 8**

Google Search   I'm Feeling Lucky

In December, Google confirmed that they were using social signals in their algorithm to help determine ranking. These included Twitter and Facebook.

Changes in 2011

This was a huge year in SEO, shocking many webmasters.

At the beginning of the year, Google tried to hit scraper sites (sites that used bots to steal and post content from other sites). This was all about trying to attribute ownership of content to the correct owner, and penalize the thieves.

On 23rd February, Panda was launched in the US. Panda (also called "Farmer") was essentially targeting low quality content and link farms (sites that were basically set up to link out to other sites, whether paid or free). The term "thin" content became popular, describing pages that really didn't say much, and were there purely to host adverts. Panda was all about squashing thin content, and a lot of sites were hit.

In March, Google introduced the +1 button. This was probably expected bearing in mind that Google had confirmed they used social signals in their ranking algorithm. What better signals to monitor than their own?

In April 2011, Panda 2.0 was released, expanding its reach to all countries of the world, though still just pages in English. More signals were included in Panda 2.0, and probably included user feedback via the Chrome web browser (users were able to "block" pages in the SERPs that they didn't like).

As if these two Panda releases were not enough, Google went on to release Panda 2.1, 2.2, 2.3, 2.4, 2.5 & 3.1, all in 2011. Note that Panda 3.0 is missing. There was an update between 2.5 and 3.1, but it is commonly referred to as Panda "Flux". Each update built on the previous one, to help eliminate low quality content from the SERPs. With each new release of Panda, webmasters worried, panicked and complained on forums. A lot of websites were penalized.

In June 2011, we saw the birth of Google's social network, Google Plus.

Another change that angered webmasters was "query encryption" in October 2011. Google said they were doing this for privacy reasons, but webmasters were suspicious of the motives. Prior to this, whenever someone searched for something at Google, the search term they typed in was passed to the site they clicked through to. That meant webmasters could see what search terms visitors were using to find their site. Query encryption changed this. Anyone that was logged into their Google account at the time they did a search would have their search query encrypted. This prevented their search term from being passed to the website they visited. The result of this was that webmasters increasingly did not know which terms people were using to find their site.

In November 2011 there was a freshness update, supposedly rewarding sites that provided time-sensitive information (like news sites), when visitors were asking for time-sensitive information.

Changes in 2012

Again, 2012 was a massive year for SEOs and webmasters. There were a huge number of prominent changes starting off with one called "Search + your World" in January. This was an aggressive measure by Google to integrate its Google+ social data and user profiles into the SERPs.

Over the year, Google released more than a dozen Panda updates, all aimed at reducing low quality pages appearing in the SERPs.

In January, Google announced a page layout algorithm change that penalized pages with too many adverts (or very little value) above the fold (above the fold refers to the visible portion of a web page when a visitor lands on the page, without scrolling down). Some SEOs referred to this as the "Top Heavy" update.

In February, Google announced another 17 changes to its algorithm, including spell-checking, which is of particular interest to us. Later in February, Google announced another 40 changes, and then in March there were 50 more changes announced, including one that made changes to anchor-text "scoring".

Google certainly weren't resting on their laurels. On April 24th, 2012, Penguin was released. This was widely expected, and webmasters assumed it was going to be an over-optimization penalty. Google initially called it a "webspam update", but it was soon named "Penguin". This update checked for a wide variety of spam techniques, including keyword stuffing, but also analyzed the anchor text used in links pointing at a website.

In April, another set of updates were announced, 52 this time.

In May, Google started rolling out "Knowledge Graph". This was a huge step towards semantic search. We also saw Penguin 1.1 this month and another 39 announced changes, including better link scheme detection (where webmasters were fabricating links to gain better rankings).

In July, Google sent out "unnatural link warnings" via Google Webmaster Tools, to any site where they had detected a large number of "unnatural" links. To avoid a penalty, Google wanted the unnatural links removed.

Think of unnatural links as any link the webmaster controls, and probably created themselves. These included links on blog networks and other low quality websites. These inbound links typically used high percentages of specific keyword phrases in the anchor text. Google wanted webmasters to be responsible for the links that pointed to their sites, and that meant webmasters were expected to contact sites that "unnaturally" linked to them, and ask for these links to be removed.

Unfortunately, if you have ever tried to contact a webmaster to ask for a link to be removed, you'll know that it can be an impossible task. For many webmasters, this was an impossible task, since the unnatural link warnings were often the result of tens or hundreds of thousands of bad links to a single site. Google eventually backtracked and said that these unnatural link warnings may not result in a penalty. The word on the street was that Google would be releasing a tool to help webmasters clean up their link profiles.

Also this month, Google announced a further 86 changes to their algorithm.

In August, Google started penalizing sites that had repeatedly violated copyright, possibly via DMCA takedown requests.

In September, another major update occurred, called the EMD update. You'll remember that EMD stands for Exact Match Domain, and refers to a domain that exactly matches a keyword phrase the site wants to rank for. We looked at these earlier. EMDs had a massive ranking advantage simply because they used the keyword phrase in the domain name. This update removed that advantage.

In October, Google announced that there were 65 changes in the previous two months.

On October 5th, there was a major update to Penguin and probably expanded Penguin's influence to non-English content.

In October, Google announced the Disavow tool. This was Google's answer to the "unnatural links" problem and completely shifted the responsibility of unnatural links onto the webmaster, by giving them a tool to "disavow" those links. If there were links from bad neighbourhoods pointing to your site, and you could not get them removed, you could disavow the links, effectively rendering them harmless.

Also in October, Google released an update to their "Page Layout" update and then finally, in December, they updated the Knowledge Graph to include non-English queries in a number of the more popular languages.

Changes in 2013

In 2013, Google updated both Panda and Penguin several times. These updates refined the two different technologies to try to increase the quality of pages ranking in the SERPs. On July 18th, a Panda update was thought to have been released to "soften" the effects of a previously released Panda, so Google obviously watched the effects of the updates, and modified them accordingly.

In June, Google released the "Payday Loan" update which targeted niches with notoriously spammy SERPs. These niches were often highly commercial, offering great rewards for any page that could rank highly, so they were targeted by spammers. Google gave the example of "payday loans" when announcing this update, hence its name.

In July, we saw an expansion of the Knowledge Graph.

Around the 20th of August, Hummingbird was released, though it wasn't announced to the SEO community until September 26th. Hummingbird seemed to be related to semantic search, trying to provide more personalized, relevant search results to each user, based on online activity, location, search history, etc.

In December 2013 there was a drop in authorship and rich snippets displayed in the SERPs (where Google displayed a photo of the author and/or other information next to the listing), as Google tightened up their criteria for showing these next to a listing.

Changes in 2014

In February, Google updated their page layout update.

In May, Payday Loan 2.0 was released. This was an update to the original Payday Loan algorithm, and it is thought to have extended the reach of this algorithm to international queries.

In May, Panda was updated (called Panda 4.0).

That brings us up to the current date that I am writing this book. As you can see, Google have been very active in trying to combat the spam thrown at them. The two major updates that most webmasters worry about are Panda and Penguin. Together, these two technologies weed out low quality pages, and pages that have been engineered to rank highly in the search engines.

That last sentence is shocking to many webmasters.

Anyone that builds a website will want it to rank well in Google, because without that, the site won't get much traffic. Therefore, webmasters WILL try to boost their rankings, and the traditional way is by working on the "on-page SEO" and inbound links. However, over the last couple of years in particular, Google have introduced measures that try to penalize any webmaster that is actively trying to boost rankings via traditional SEO.

Google want the best pages to rank at the top of the SERPs. Google want to reward the pages that deserve to be at the top, rather than the pages that webmasters force to the top using SEO (much of which Google collectively calls "webspam").

What this means to you, is that you have to deliver the absolute best quality content you can. You need to create content that deserves to be at the top of Google.

Fortunately, Google do offer us a lot of advice on how to create the type of content they want in their SERPs. In fact, they have set up a web page called "Webmaster Guidelines" to tell us exactly what they want, and what they don't want. We'll look at this shortly, but first, let's see how we used to create content.

How we used to write content

Let's have a look at how content used to be written. Armed with the knowledge of the previous section, you should be able to easily spot why those techniques no longer work.

I'll show you an example article in a minute – one that used to rank well in Google, and was quite profitable through Adsense advertising. First, let me walk you through the process that was used to write the article (the same process millions of webmasters used, and some still do, to create their webspam).

Step 1 – Identify profitable keyword phrases.

This was (and still is) fairly easy using any number of keyword tools. Keywords could be sorted and filtered to show those that were in high demand (being searched for a lot), yet had low competition (not many web pages targeted those phrases). It was then just a case of seeing how much an advertiser would have to pay to bid on that keyword in the Google Adwords program (so their ads appeared in the Google search results). Those that commanded the higher fees were potentially the most profitable.

Step 2 – Write an article based around that keyword phrase in the hope that it would rank well for that, and usually only that, keyword phrase. The keyword phrase was typically placed in the title, the body of the article a few times (let's say a density of 4%), etc, and a couple of synonyms were added, if possible.

A page created this way had the potential to rank high, and get traffic.

A lot of "Internet Marketers" used this as their business model, creating dozens, even hundreds or thousands of websites (using tools in many cases to automate the site building) with lots of pages targeting individual, high demand phrases. By slapping up several Adsense adverts on their pages, they could monetize that traffic and make money from their websites. As you can imagine, the level of spam in the Google index skyrocketed.

Here is a real example of a piece of contact that was written well before Panda and Penguin, ranked well, and made a fair bit of money through Google Adsense.

Special Effects Contact Lenses

Have you seen star of the movie Riddick Chronicles? Bet you've wondered for the longest time where to get his obviously special contact lenses. Films and the costume industry need to employ a lot of special effects to make the character more convincing, and special effects contact lenses, help to achieve these look. But special effects contact lenses are medical devices too and that means great care must be used in buying and wearing them.

Since special effects contacts are medical devices, under FDA law, any purchaser must be fitted for them before he or she can use these. Even if you have 20/20, vision or possess a mild case of astigmatism. .

Examples of special effects lenses are: Wild Eyes Zebra, Pool Shark 8 Ball, Starry eyes (have the stars and moon in your pupils), The Stars & Stripes: an American flag, Red Spiral: red with a white spiral, Fire: yellow flames circle your pupil on a red background or Bloodshot: white with red "blood vessels".

Special effects contacts are made out of soft lenses and worn according to different replacement schedules, such as:

Daily wear lenses - These lenses must be removed at the end of each day, cleaned and then stored.

Extended wear soft lenses - designed to be worn for periods up to a month and can be worn even when sleeping.

Disposable contact lenses - worn for a specified time and then thrown away.

So whether you just like to show your patriotism during the celebration of Independence Day, or change a mood, special effects contacts can do that for you with punctuation.

However, you must never share or swap your costume contacts with anybody. An eye infection caused by improper use can lead to blindness.

Get fitted for your prescription, for it the contact lenses don't fit your eyes properly, it could lead to serious eye problems, scarring, abrasions and infections.

As long as you follow the rules in buying special effect lenses and take care of the ones you have, you won't have to worry a thing about wearing them. So make sure you go to a trained eye professional for your contacts.

That is 363 words.

Read it and see what you think.

Is this a good article?

Does it read naturally?

Can you see what phrase the author was trying to rank for?

The webmaster was clearly trying to target the phrase "special effects contact lenses". The article included:

- **Special effects contact lenses** in the title and twice in the opening paragraph.
- **Special effects contacts** THREE times.
- **Special effects** SEVEN times in the article and once more in the title.

Overall:

- **Special** appeared NINE times on the page.
- **Effect(s)** appeared NINE times on the page.
- **Contact(s)** appeared ELEVEN times on the page.
- **Lenses** appeared TWELVE times on the page.

And this was actually one of the better pieces of keyword-focused content that I saw ranking in Google!

This article is clearly very poor. It's not just that it is obviously focused on a specific keyword phrase, the article also suffers from poor grammar throughout. To me, it reads as if someone was given a keyword phrase, and asked to fill in a bunch of words around that phrase ;)

Though badly written, the article isn't all bad. It does actually include some useful information. Overall though, I am sure you agree that you would not expect to read that article in a newspaper or magazine discussing special effects contact lenses, would you?

Google have actually stated in their guidelines that one of the tests you can apply to your content is whether or not it would be out of place in a quality magazine.

I have a different test for my own content. I ask myself, *would visitors want to share this content?*

In other words, is the content "Share Bait". We'll come back to this term later in the book.

The Webmaster Guidelines

So you want to be in Google?

Then Follow Google's Rules....

You can find them here:

https://support.google.com/webmasters/answer/35769?hl=en

If you don't want to have to read through all of the guidelines, or this chapter, I can summarize what Google want in terms of content in one sentence.

Create content your visitors want to see!

Google can gauge how successful you are in that goal, because they monitor a number of factors including:

- How long a visitor stays on your page/site
- The bounce rate of your pages (the percentage of people that bounce straight back to Google after visiting your page).
- How many citations/shares your page(s) gets from social networks like Twitter, Facebook and especially Google Plus.

Obviously content is only one part of the jigsaw puzzle. You can have great content but break some of the other rules in the Webmaster Guidelines. Do that and you are just as likely to lose rankings and disappear from the SERPs. For that reason alone, I recommend you read this chapter in full, and refer back to the Google guidelines regularly, as they are updated occasionally.

A Breakdown of the Google Webmaster Guidelines

The guidelines cover more than just creating good content. They are there to tell you the best ways to help Google "find, crawl and index your site" as well as the "quality" aspects. The guidelines also give specific examples of what they consider "illicit" practices that could lead to a site being penalized or even removed (de-indexed) from Google.

The guidelines are split up into three main sections:

1. Design and content guidelines
2. Technical guidelines
3. Quality guidelines

Let's go through some of the more important points in each of these three sections.

Design and Content Guidelines

- "Include a sitemap on your site." A sitemap should link to the most important pages on your site, in fact, every page that you want Google to know about.
- "Every page on your site should be reachable via at least one static text link on another page." I'd actually go one step further and suggest that you make sure every page on your site is only two clicks away from the homepage.
- "Don't have too many links on a page." How many is too many? That's difficult to answer, but I would certainly stay away from long sidebar menus listing dozens of other pages on your site.
- "Create a useful, information-rich site."
- "Think about words users would type to find your pages, and make sure that your site actually includes those words within it." This is one instruction that I think is left over from the pre-Panda and pre-Penguin Google. As we saw earlier in the book, a lot of top pages that rank for a phrase do not include that phrase on the page. I think it is important to include all of the words that make up a phrase, but having the exact phrase is unnecessary.
- "Try to use text instead of images to display important names, content or links. The Google crawler does not recognise text contained in images." Google want to accurately assess your content and categorize it. It should make sense that important text is written as text, rather than as part of an image. However, there may be times you will want to add text as an image, for example, when displaying a contact email address. This prevents bots from harvesting your email address and selling it to spam lists, which ultimately results in unsolicited emails, usually with no way to stop them.
- "Make sure that your <title> and ALT attributes are descriptive and accurate." A lot of webmasters use the title tags and ALT tags as a way of inserting more keyword phrases into a page. Don't do it. Not only does Google see this "keyword stuffing" as "webspam", but it also deprives your blind and visually impaired visitors from accurately "reading" your web page.

Technical Guidelines

A lot of these technical guidelines are for advanced webmasters, though there are a few that everyone should be concerned about. Here they are:

1. Search engine spiders tend to see web content as text, so things like Flash, Javascript, etc, can cause problems. If you want your content spidered and indexed, make sure it is readable as plain text. Google point out that you can

check to see what a typical search engine spider sees, by visiting your site in a text browser like Lynx (http://lynx.browser.org/).

2. "Test your site to make sure that it appears correctly in different browsers." This is quite important because quite often, what we are seeing in one browser is not how another browser displays the page. There are a number of free online tools that can help you test this. Just search Google for "test site in different browsers". Don't forget, an increasing number of visitors will be using mobile devices like tablets and phones which have very different screen resolutions, and don't forget that some of these are not able to display flash video.

3. "Monitor your site's performance and optimize load times." Google suggest that load time is a factor in their ranking algorithm. Any page that takes too long to load could be penalized. A long load time WILL annoy visitors, which may get them clicking the back button before your page loads. This of course will be noticed by Google if the visitor bounces right back to the Google search results to find a different web page. There are a number of free online tools that can analyze your page load times. The free one that I use is at http://GTMetrix.com.

Quality Guidelines

The quality guidelines cover the more common forms of "deceptive and manipulative behavior" to avoid. However, as Google point out, just because something is not listed in this section, does not mean it is safe. This section is well summarized by this sentence from the quality guidelines.

"Webmasters who spend their energies upholding the spirit of the basic principles will provide a much better user experience and subsequently enjoy better ranking than those who spend their time looking for loopholes they can exploit."

By looking at what not to do, we can get a good idea of what Google actually want. Many of these things will come as no surprise after we saw the long list of Google algorithm changes earlier.

Before we look at the list of what not to do, Google do offer a few points on what they DO want us to do. They are:

1. "Make pages primarily for users, not for search engines." Remember that special effects contact lenses article? Was that written for the user or the search engine? That article is exactly what Google do not want, and writing content by focusing on a specific keyword phrase is only going to cause you problems.

2. "Don't deceive your users." This is a wide ranging statement that covers a whole host of sins. We will see examples of this in a moment.
3. "Avoid tricks intended to improve search engine rankings." Google suggest you ask yourself "Does this help my users? Would I do this if search engines didn't exist?" If the answer is no, don't do it. I certainly would not feel happy showing the special effects contact lens article to a Google employee as an example of my site content, would you?
4. "Think about what makes your website unique, valuable, or engaging. Make your website stand out from others in your field." This is probably one of the more important things to remember. If you want your page to rank number one in Google, does it deserve to? How is your page better than the pages already ranked in the top 10? What does your page add? What makes it unique and valuable enough that Google have to include it in the top 10?

OK, so those are the guidelines on what Google actually want. Now let's look at a few of the examples they specifically mention for things to avoid.

Things Not To Do
1. **Automatically generate content**. This is content that has been created by some form of computer program or script. An example that may seem less obvious is to take your English article and use a software program to convert that in Spanish, German and French, and then post that content on your site to offer your visitors different languages. There is nothing to stop you using a translator tool to create an initial draft in another language, but you must get someone proficient in that language to go through and make changes so that it is actually grammatical correct. Another example that saw a rise in popularity a few years ago (and is still done by many today), is spinning articles. This is a process whereby one article is spun into different versions using a tool that swaps out synonyms, sentences, and even whole paragraphs.
2. **Link Schemes**. The term "link scheme" covers a multitude of sins, but basically includes "Any links intended to manipulate PageRank or a site's ranking in Google search results". We all know that links help a page to rank in the SERPs. Therefore webmasters have come up with all manner of "link schemes" to build backlinks, increase their rankings and increase profits. Link schemes include buying/bribing and selling links, link exchanges, large scale article marketing or guest posting with keyword rich anchor text links, and using automated software to build links. In fact, any link that was not "editorially placed or vouched for by the site's owner" is considered an unnatural link. Remember those?

3. **Cloaking (and sneaky redirects)**. This is a way of deceiving both the visitor and the search engines. It is essentially presenting one version of a page to the search engines (which is highly optimized to rank well), but when the link in the SERPs is clicked, the user is redirected to a completely different page (which isn't so highly optimized and therefore would not have ranked so well in the search engine).

4. **Hidden text or links**. Using CSS (a technology that helps us control how our web pages look in a browser), it is quite easy to make text the same colour as the background (for example white text on a white background), effectively making it invisible. This was a technique that some people used to stuff keyword phrases into their pages in the hope that their page would rank for those phrases. The search engine spiders would see the keywords, since they are viewing a text based version of the page, but human visitors would not see the keywords. Hidden links were often used to manipulate Page Rank and ultimately rankings.

5. **Doorway pages**. This is still used a lot today. The webmaster sets up a large number of pages, each trying to rank for a specific term. The special effects contact lenses article we saw earlier was an example of a doorway page. That contact lens site targeted hundreds of keyword phrases, each one on a separate web page. A twist on the doorway page idea is where all of the doorway pages are on separate websites, and they all link to a single web page or sales letter on a different website. The idea here is to funnel the doorway traffic to a single sales page. This system helped spread the risk, because if one doorway page (and the domain it was on) got penalized, the others were still safely working away, funneling that traffic (and Page Rank) to the main sales page.

6. **Scraped Content**. This is where a webmaster took content from one site and posted it on their own site. Software tools were often employed to do this job. The idea was to increase the amount of content on a website in the hope that this increased the number of terms the site ranked for, therefore bringing in more traffic and increasing profits. While some content scrapers stole complete articles, even entire websites, and therefore infringed copyright, others stayed within the law and were a little less aggressive. For example, a webmaster might grab videos from Youtube and embed them into pages on his own site. That is within the terms of Youtube, so isn't stealing content. However, just embedding the video in a new web page is not enough to satisfy Google, because the video is already available on Youtube. Why do we need a second copy? The webmaster MUST add significant value to any content

"scraped" from another site. In the Youtube video example, this would mean adding original thought, opinion and commentary to the web page.

7. **Thin affiliate site**s. Affiliate sites can be a great way to make a second (or even primary) income. You place adverts on your site, and if someone buys something through your link, you make a commission. However, if you run an affiliate site, you MUST add significant value for your visitor. You cannot just throw up pages and pages of affiliate product "reviews" containing nothing by copied product descriptions, copied reviews, an image or two and an affiliate link. Google want you to add your own unique and original content to the pages. Google state in their guidelines that "Affiliate program content should form only a small part of the content of your site". Does your site offer anything that the original merchant site does not?

8. **Keyword Stuffing**. This is where a page has words, phrases or numbers added, purely in an attempt to manipulate web page ranking. For example, if you had a website on teeth whitening, and included a list of the US states in the hope of ranking for "teeth whitening California", "teeth whitening Utah", "teeth whitening Kansas", etc, then that is keyword stuffing, and Google will penalize you when they find it.

9. **Preventing and removing user-generated spam**. If you run a Wordpress site, then chances are you'll be accepting comments from visitors. A lot of comments will only be written by people looking for a link back to their own website, and many people use software tools to create hundreds or thousands of comments on any blog that accepts them. Never EVER approve a comment that does not add value to the page on your site. Certainly don't approve those comments that attempt to flatter you with "Great site", or "Wow, I learned a lot". They are clearly spam comments that are trying to appeal to your ego to get them approved. If you run any type of site that offers visitors a profile page, or a forum, you need to keep those clean as well. Low quality profile pages (as generated by spammers and their software tools), as well as spammy forum posts are YOUR responsibility if they are on your site, and Google will penalize YOU for them.

That covers the webmaster guidelines. Hopefully you aren't feeling daunted by that long list of don'ts. As you can see, Google are serious about making their search engine results the best they can be, and if you want to see your pages ranking in the SERPs, you need to take these guidelines seriously. It actually isn't that difficult. Just remember a couple of simple rules.

1. Create your site and content for your visitor, not for the search engines.
2. Don't do something you wouldn't otherwise do if search engines did not exist.

OK, let's look at how we can create content that the search engines will love. To do that, we need to create content that our visitors love, and that means we need content ideas.

What sort of content do your visitors want to see?

Finding Content Ideas

The secret to keeping Google happy is to provide your visitors with the type of content that keeps them engaged, makes them want to come back, and excites them enough that they want to tell their friends, family and social (Twitter, Facebook, etc) followers about it.

Your first job is to come up with content ideas that can satisfy these rigorous demands.

There are a number of ways to come up with this type of content, and in this chapter, I am going to go through some of the better ones.

1. Check out competitor sites

This is usually my first stop. Do a search at Google for a generic term related to your niche and then visit the top 10 sites to see what they are talking about.

If these sites have social sharing buttons, see which pieces of content have the most shares, as those are the ones that have the potential to excite your audience as well.

2. Use "footprints" to find popular content

This is one of my favourite ways of finding popular topics to write about.

A lot of websites are built using a Content Management System (CMS). A good example of a popular CMS is Wordpress. In fact, I use Wordpress exclusively on all of the websites I run.

One thing you may notice as you look at a lot of Wordpress sites is that certain phrases appear on most, or all of the pages built with the tool. This is because those phrases are hard-coded into Wordpress itself.

A good example can be seen below:

Leave a Reply

Your email address will not be published. Required fields are marked *

See that phrase "Leave a Reply"? That phrase appears on hundreds of thousands of websites built with Wordpress, just above the comments box. If I do a search on Google for "Leave a Reply" in quotes, this is what I get:

Google "leave a reply"

Web   Images   Videos   News   Maps   More ▾   Search tools

About 143,000,000 results (0.75 seconds)

Google tells me that there are "about 143 million" pages that have that exact phrase on the page.

Now, in terms of finding content ideas, this footprint is not very useful. However, there is a related footprint that is pure gold.

Check out these screenshots:

299 RESPONSES TO "GREEN SMOOTHIE 101: HOW TO MAKE A GREEN SMOOTHIE"

405 Responses to The Secret Ingredient In Your Orange Juice

221 Responses to "The Trembling Kind"

These screenshots are from three pages on three different websites. See how each one has "XXX responses to".

Each response is a comment, and the more comments an article has, the more interesting that article probably is to the target audience.

So how can we use this as a "footprint" to find popular content?

"Responses to" on its own isn't much good as a footprint, since we only want to find pages that have a lot of responses.

34

However, using a little trick of the trade, we can modify the "responses to", to include a number range like this:

"50..500 Responses to"

If you search for this in Google, the search engine returns pages that have anywhere from 50 to 500 "responses to". Cool eh?

I've used 50..500 as my number range, but you could change this to 100..1000 or whatever you want. It will all depend on your niche and how many results Google is finding for your footprints. In less popular niches, you may need to reduce your lower limit to something like 20 or 25.

Now, the footprint we've just talked about isn't much use on its own. We need to tell Google that we are only interested in pages related to our niche. Let's look at a specific example.

Let's say I have a website on weight loss.

I would select a few generic keyword phrases for my niche like "weight loss", "lose weight", "lose fat" and maybe even "diet", and then build footprints, like this:

"weight loss" "50..500 Responses to"

"lose weight" "50..500 Responses to"

"lose fat" "50..500 Responses to"

"diet" "50..500 Responses to"

I would then visit Google and type these into the search box. Let's take the first one and do that now.

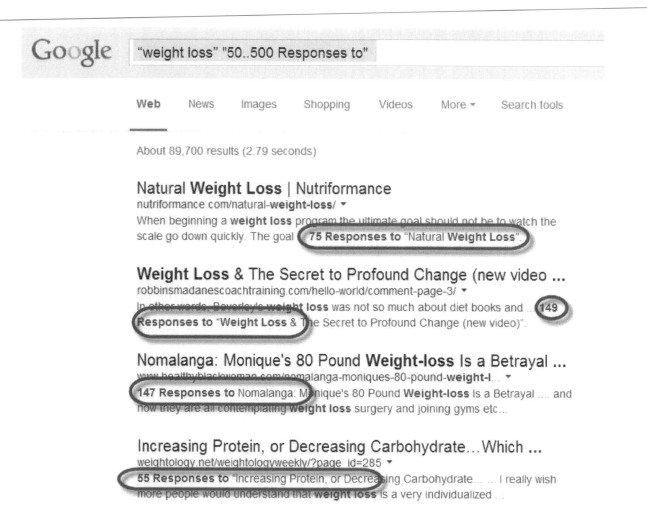

Google highlights the phrases in our search term, so we can instantly see that these results have 75, 149, 147 and 55 responses respectively. Those responses are comments to the original post, and represent visitor interaction on the site. Not only could you go to these popular posts and leave your own comments, which would raise awareness for your own website, but you could also check out the topic of the post, work out why it is so interesting to those visitors, and write a similar post on your own site.

Here's an idea. If a post is a little controversial, why not write an opposing view on your own site, and then post a comment on this original post mentioning your opposing view with a link. Assuming your comment was approved, that would not only provide a link to your site, but also give you potential visitors interested in seeing your opinions on the topic. People who commented on the original post are more likely to comment on your post, whether they agree or disagree with your point of view. Since Google loves to see posts with comments, that will kick start your own rankings.

Another footprint that I like, which often returns even more results is this one:

"50..500 comments"

We use it in exactly the same way, and this will turn up good numbers of posts to investigate. Here is a comparison of the two footprints for our "weight loss" example.

"weight loss" "50..500 Responses to"

Web   News   Images   Shopping   Videos

About 89,700 results (2.79 seconds)

"weight loss" "50..500 comments"

Web   News   Images   Videos   Shopping

About 3,880,000 results (1.11 seconds)

The "responses to" gave use 89,700 results to work with. The "comments" footprint gave us nearly 4 millions.

You can of course use this footprint technique to find popular posts on specific topics. For example, suppose you had a health site, and wanted to write an article or two on kale (the vegetable).

This footprint technique would give you ideas on what type of article would be of interest:

"kale" "50..500 comments"   🎤

Web   Images   News   Videos   Shopping   More ▾   Search tools

About 1,350,000 results (0.88 seconds)

6 Tips for Flawless Kale Chips + All-Dressed Kale Chips ...

ohsheglows.com/.../6-tips-for-flawless-kale-chips-all-dressed-kal... ▾
by Angela Liddon - in 1,556 Google+ circles
Mar 12, 2014 - It took me a while to master my baked kale chip recipe, but I've
learned some valuable lessons ... **98 comments**... read them below or add one
}.

Recipe: Weeknight Mushroom and Kale Pasta - 100 Days of ...

www.100daysofrealfood.com/.../recipe-weeknight-mushroo... ▾
★★★★★ Rating: 4.8 - 23 reviews
Jan 6, 2014 - Turn the heat back down to medium and add the heavy
cream, kale, salt, ... **137 comments** to Recipe: Weeknight Mushroom and
Kale Pasta.
More by Lisa Leake - in 362 Google+ circles

Recipe: Kale and Apple Salad - 100 Days of Real Food
www.100daysofrealfood.com/.../recipe-kale-and-apple-sala... ▾
★★★★★ Rating: 5 - 4 reviews
Nov 22, 2013 - This kale and apple salad may be just for the adult table
though, if I am being honest. I don't ... **56 comments** to Recipe: Kale and
Apple Salad.
More by Lisa Leake - in 362 Google+ circles

That's three different ideas for articles in the first three results – kale chips, kale
pasta and kale salad. Best of all, they are all popular articles.

You could use this type of footprint technique to build up sections on your website, or
even find complete niche website ideas!

3. Forums

Forums are always a great place to find content ideas, after all, people visit forums to
discuss ideas and ask for answers to their problems.

You could start off with a simple Google search like:

"weight loss" "forum"

By enclosing both parts of the search string in quotes, Google will only return pages that have both of those strings on the page.

Here is that search in Google:

"weight loss" "forum"

| Web | Shopping | Videos | News | Images | More ▾ | Search tools |

About 46,000,000 results (0.58 seconds)

Weight Loss Forum
weight-loss.fitness.com/ ▾
Weight loss Forum.com - free weightloss community. Discuss weightloss and diet ideas with other people. View other success stories and find your motivation.
First - Newcomers - Before & After ... and In-Between - Weight Loss Programs

General Diet and Weight Loss Help - Free Diet and Fitness ...
www.myfitnesspal.com/forums/.../9-general-diet-and-weigh... ▾ MyFitnessPal ▾
General Diet and Weight Loss Help at the MyFitnessPal diet and exercise forums. ...
NEW FORUM GUIDELINES - PLEASE READ BEFORE POSTING · Steven. 1.
Calorie Counter - Newbies Please READ ME - Links in MFP you want to read ...

46 million pages contain the phrase "weight loss" and the word "forum". That's quite a good start and will be good enough for most popular niches. However, that search does not guarantee that the results are actual forums, just that the word "forum" appears on the page.

To increase your chances of finding real forums in your niche, you can again use footprints. Forums are created using scripts, and scripts leave footprints that we can use.

Here are some footprints to try in combination with your generic niche term:

"weight loss" "viewtopic"

"weight loss" "Powered by PHPbb"

"weight loss" "Powered by vBulletin"

There are other footprints, but these should be enough to get you started.

When you get to the forums, look so see what questions people are asking. If there is a question with a lot of replies, or obvious interest, consider writing an article for your site on that topic, then join the forum and direct people to your post. Normal forum etiquette means you should not be joining a forum just to link to pages on your own site. You'll be seen as a spammer, but if you join relevant forums, post helpful responses to questions, and ask interesting questions to interact with others, you will eventually be able to link to articles on your own site (or any other site) without being seen as a spammer.

Another footprint that can yield good results is the word "community". After all, communities are groups of like minded people discussing a topic of interest.

"weight loss" "community"

Web   News   Shopping   Videos   Images   More ▾   Search tools

About 115,000,000 results (0.61 seconds)

Weight Loss Blogs From The MyFitnessPal Community ...
www.myfitnesspal.com/blog/popular ▾ MyFitnessPal ▾
Honestly, **weight loss** surgery is not for everyone, but I could not have asked for a better outcome. I have been so lucky and blessed. I don't exagerate one bit ...

Weight Loss Community at traineo | Weight Loss Forum ...
www.traineo.com/ ▾
Use traineo's powerful online tools designed by **weight loss** experts to ... and then join thousands of active **community** members sharing motivation and support ...

This won't always give you real communities, but it usually does turn up some gems that you can mine for content ideas.

4. Q & A sites

What better place to find ideas for content than websites set up to ask and answer questions? There are several sites like this, including:

- Ask (http://Ask.com)
- Yahoo Answers (https://answers.yahoo.com/)
- Quora (https://www.quora.com/).

Quora is my personal favourite. You can type in just about anything at Quora, to find real questions & answers.

Sign up for Quora (it's free), and you can start to join the community and offer help to others. It's a great way to drum up some interest in your website.

There is a search box at the top of the screen, where you can type in your topic of interest:

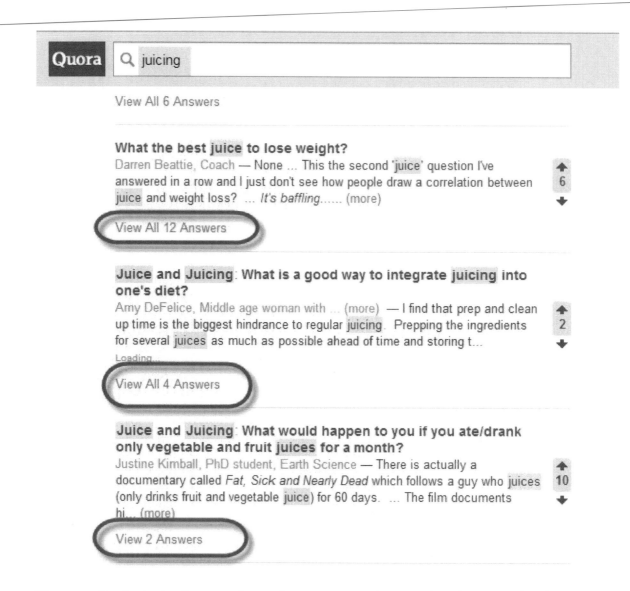

The results include the number of answers each question has received, so you can quickly gauge interaction with each question. If you click through to a question, you can get even more valuable data:

Question Stats

Latest activity was 31 Mar

This question has **1** monitor with **1183221** topic followers.

5,497 views on this question.

14 people are following this question.

You can see in the screenshot that this particular question has been viewed 5497 times, and is being followed by 14 people.

Every question is assigned to one or more topics. You can see that this question was over 1 million "topic followers". However, this question was assigned to 4 different topics – "juice and juicing", "weight loss", "fitness" and "cooking". This value of 1 million topic followers is the combined total of all 4 topics. If you want to know how many followers each topic has, you can mouse over the topics listed at the top of the page:

Look for questions that have a lot of replies, and those that have a lot of people following the question. This helps to identify popular content that you could write about on your own website.

Again, with Quora, you can post links to your own website, so there is nothing to stop you from answering a question and linking to an article on your own site ;). I see the process something like this:

1. Find a popular question.
2. Write an article for my own site that answers the question, but also offers a different point of view, or different information to that already given on the Quora site.
3. Answer the question on the Quora site, with reference to the article on your own site.

Not only does this technique add valuable content to your own website, but it can also get people interested in that topic back to your website. Again, don't abuse this or you will be seen as a spammer. I find it is better to try to help out a bit on Quora, answering the odd question before I try the "answer with link" tactic.

5. Follow RSS feeds

An RSS feed is essentially a list of pages on a web site. RSS feeds can include all pages on a site, or just the last 10 or so pages (the exact number can be controlled by the webmaster).

A lot of websites publish RSS feeds, and in fact, ALL Wordpress sites create RSS feeds automatically. A Wordpress site actually creates a number of different RSS feeds, including feeds for:

- The latest posts
- Each category
- Every tag page
- All posts by each author
- And more...

One of the best ways to find content ideas is to follow your competitor websites, and see what they are publishing content on. If they publish an RSS feed, it's easy to spy on them.

There are a number of services that can help you monitor the RSS feeds of other websites. My favourite is called Feedly, and you can sign up for a free account at Feedly.com by logging in with your Twitter, Facebook or Google Plus account.

Essentially you tell Feedly what RSS feeds you are interested in following (by providing the feed URL), and they'll keep those feeds updated in your account, so you can see the new content as it is published.

Let's do a real example.

Let's suppose I am interested in weight loss.

I can do a search at Google for weight loss RSS feeds as follows:

"weight loss" "rss"

This will find pages that include the phrase "weight loss", but also contain the word "RSS" on the page. This usually returns pages for sites that offer an RSS feed. Here are the results in Google.

"weight loss" "rss"

Web   News   Images   Shopping   Videos   More ▾   Search tools

About 71,900,000 results (0.47 seconds)

Women's Health & Fitness **RSS** Feeds
www.womenshealthandfitness.com.au/**rss** ▾
Browse workouts, **weight loss** tips, diet foods, recipes & exercises for women. ...
Subscribe to the Women's Health & Fitness **RSS** feed to get the latest content ...

Diet and **Weight Loss** News -- ScienceDaily
www.sciencedaily.com/news/health.../diet_and_**weight_loss**... ▾ Science Daily ▾
Read **weight loss** articles and the latest information on dieting. ... ScienceDaily's Diet
and **Weight Loss** News, delivered daily to your email inbox or **RSS** reader.

Obesity / **Weight Loss** / Fitness News - Medical News Today
www.medicalnewstoday.com/.../fitness-obesity ▾ Medical News Today ▾
Obesity / **Weight Loss** / Fitness News from Medical News Today - Page 1. ... Follow this
category's news on Twitter · Follow this category's news using **RSS** ...

If I click on the first item, I can search for an RSS feed which often looks like this:

Rather than click the icon, I typically right click and copy the URL, which I can then add to Feedly.

To add to Feedly, just paste the URL into the search box:

Read more, know more.

.. and hit the return key.

You will see a preview of the feed, and a +feedly button that you can click to add the feed to your account.

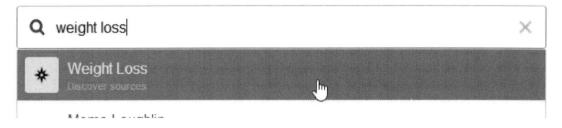

Weight Loss [+feedly]

— 1 readers

MAY 28

3 extra ways to burn fat

Need help losing weight? Here are 3 key fat burning tips from the experts. 1. Get more sleepYou're less likely to hit your maximum intensity if you feel like crawling into a hole. Melanie McGrice, from the Dietitians Association of
41 Weight Loss / by Administrator / 14d

MAY 14

Alkaline diet review

The Alkaline diet promotes a healthy pH balance within the body. But does it help with weight loss? The lowdownThe theory is that you need an optimal pH balance (balance between acid and base, also known as alkaline) in your
6 Weight Loss / by Administrator / 29d

MAY 07

5 sensible diet tips

Weight loss coach and author Sally Asher offers her top tips. 1. Eat nutritious

Once the feed is added, your account will track that feed and show you new content as it is posted to that site.

Find a number of RSS feeds and add them all to the same Feedly account. You can then track new content across a number of sites. You can even let Feedly find feeds for you by entering a keyword:

Read more, know more.

🔍 weight loss   ✕

☀ **Weight Loss**
Discover sources

This will then list a number of feeds that you can easily add to your feedly account by clicking the add button:

47

Weight Loss

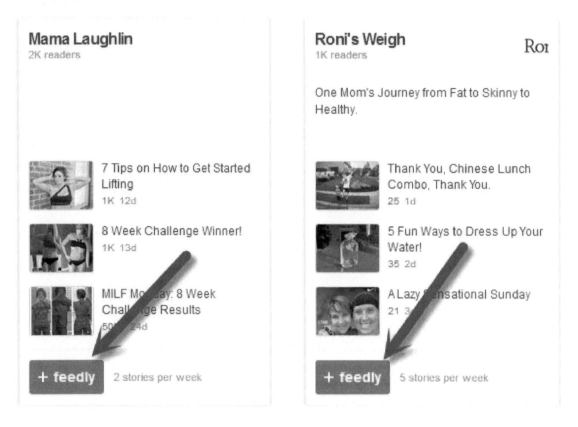

Within Feedly you can even create categories to add feeds to, so you could have a category for all "weight loss" feeds, another for "weight loss recipes", another for "diets" and so on. That way you can monitor multiple topics related to your site.

When new content is found in the feeds you are monitoring, you'll see them in your Feedly stream. You can then visit these articles, check out their popularity (social shares, comments, etc), and "borrow" popular topics to write about for your own site.

I'll leave you to explore Feedly yourself, but I'd recommend you certainly add relevant feeds from your competitors, as well as those sites at the top of the search engines for key phrases you want to rank for.

Before we leave the topic of RSS feeds, there is a special case that I wanted to mention – news feeds.

Let's take the weight loss example again.

Over on Google, you need to sign into your Google account (your gmail account if you have one, if not, create one).

OK, if I search for weight loss, I get this:

Notice that menu underneath the search box? One of those items is "News", and by clicking it, you can find relevant, up to the minute (usually) news on your chosen search phrase.

You can see that the first item was posted 15 hours previously, and the next one 16 hours before I searched. That's pretty up-to-date, and if you have a section on your site to show "current news" in your niche, this information can be invaluable.

Google News used to offer an RSS feed for these results pages, but they stopped doing that. However, if you scroll to the bottom of the page, you should see a button to "Create Alert".

Click it.

On the left of the screen that loads, you can set up your Alert:

Alerts

Search query:	weight loss
Result type:	News ↕
Language:	English ↕
Region:	Any Region ↕
How often:	As-it-happens ↕
How many:	Only the best results ↕
Deliver to:	Feed ↕

CREATE ALERT   Manage your alerts

Make sure you set the "Deliver to" field to Feed.

You can see a preview of your feed on the right, so you can modify these settings to get the best possible feed for your needs. For example, you might alter the search query a little, or select a specific country.

When you are happy with your feed results, click the "Create Alert" button.

Google will now show you a list of all alerts that you have set up. Next to each alert is a feed link and icon. Click the feed link and then copy the URL from your browser address bar.

You can now paste this URL into Feedly to monitor Google news for niche related stories.

Feedly and RSS feeds can keep you up-to-date in your niche, and you'll always hear about the hot topics as they arise. This can be a great way to identify content ideas that are sure to keep your visitors happy.

6. Keyword Research - Using Google Keyword Planner

I was a little reluctant to talk about keyword research tools as a way to find content ideas, for one simple reason. Armed with the data from a keyword research session, the temptation to create "webspam" is too hard to resist for many. Keyword research tools are one of the main reasons Google has had to go to extreme measures to clean up their search results of poor, thin content.

For years, the process employed by many internet marketers was the same:

1. Do keyword research.
2. Find keywords that are searched for a lot, have low competition and are commercial terms that are expensive to advertise on Google Adwords.
3. Write a page of content around each of these profitable keywords.
4. Slap up Google Adsense on the page.

That was the recipe for many people to make big money online. A single web page ranking high in Google could make 10s or even 100s of dollars a day with Google Adsense clicks. You can see why the temptation was there to get as many pages online as possible, and some webmasters literally put up millions of pages.

With that said, keyword research is still a valuable way to find out what people want. Like so many things, it's how you use the data that will decide whether Google see you as a great content creator or web spammer.

Google's own keyword research tool is free to use, though you will need a Google Adwords account. Fortunately, you can sign up for an Adwords account without having to give a credit card.

You can find the Google Keyword Planner here:

https://adwords.google.com/KeywordPlanner

If necessary, sign up for an Adwords account. This is currently as simple as signing into Google with your Gmail address and following the simple prompts.

You'll get a message saying Welcome to Adwords, and a prompt to go and enter your billing data. Ignore that, and use the menu at the top to navigate to the Keyword Planner.

/ords or group them into ad groups

I'm not going to show you everything you can do in the Google Keyword Planner, but I'll show you enough to get you started.

Once you are logged in, you may notice a warning at the top asking you to complete your set up of your account. You can ignore that.

There are a few menu choices on the left:

Keyword Planner
Plan your next search campaign

What would you like to do?

▸ Search for new keyword and ad group ideas

▸ Get search volume for a list of keywords or group them into ad groups

▸ Get traffic estimates for a list of keywords

▸ Multiply keyword lists to get new keyword ideas

The one we are interested in is at the top – **Search for new keyword and ad group ideas**, so click it.

You'll now be presented with a form to fill out, to tell Google what you want to do.

What would you like to do?

▼ Search for new keyword and ad group ideas

Enter one or more of the following:

Your product or service

weight loss

Your landing page

www.example.com/page

Your product category

Enter or select a product category ▼

Targeting [?]

United States

All languages

Google

Negative keywords

Date range [?]

Show avg. monthly searches
for: Last 12 months

Customize your search [?]

Keyword filters

Keyword options
Show broadly related ideas
Hide keywords in my account
Hide keywords in my plan

Include/Exclude

Get ideas

In the "Your product or service" box, enter a word or phrase that is highly relevant to the topic of your website.

Leave everything else alone.

Click the "Get Ideas" button.

54

The data that is returned is on two separate tabs - "Ad Group Ideas" and "Keyword Ideas".

| Ad group ideas | Keyword ideas | | | | | ↓ Download | Add all (47) |

Ad group (by relevance)	Keywords		Avg. monthly searches [?]	Competition [?]	Suggested bid [?]	Ad impr. share [?]	Add to plan
Loss Fast (14)	fast weight loss,...	⌶	30,010	Medium	€2.90	0%	»
Plan For Weight...	weight loss plan...	⌶	48,830	Medium	€3.33	0%	»
Diet Weight (24)	weight loss diet,...	⌶	24,160	Medium	€2.65	0%	»
Supplements Fo...	weight loss sup...	⌶	53,170	High	€1.66	0%	»
Best Weight (19)	best weight loss...	⌶	50,100	Medium	€3.03	0%	»

All of this data is designed by Google to help people that want to buy advertising, but it is still very useful for us. The Ad Group Ideas are collections of related keyword phrases. Google groups them to help advertisers, but these groups can often give us ideas on content, or even site design. I often find ideas in the Ad Groups for new categories of content on my own site.

However, I really want to see the phrases people are typing into Google to find content. We can do this by clicking over to the "Keyword Ideas" tab.

At the very top of this screen, we can see the data for the exact phrase that I typed in:

| Ad group ideas | Keyword ideas | | | ⌶ | ↓ |

Search terms		Avg. monthly searches [?]	Competition [?]	Suggested bid [?]	A
weight loss	⌶	90,500	High	€3.28	

Th

e exact term "weight loss" is searched for around 90,500 times a month. I can also see that competition is high (lots of advertisers bidding on this phrase), and Google is recommending I bid €3.28.

What does bidding €3.28 mean?

If someone searches Google for "weight loss" and Google show my advert, they want me to agree to pay up to €3.28 if that person clicks on my ad. That's €3.28 PER CLICK!

Ads can appear in the search results, or on partner sites (and pretty much anyone can be a partner through the Adsense program). Imagine you had a weight loss site and added Adsense to monetize it. If there are advertisers willing to pay €3.28 per click, then every time a visitor on your site clicked this type of advert, you would make a "commission" equal to the lions share of up to €3.28. Can you see why people started creating pages around specific keyword phrases?

Below the data for your seed term, you will see a lot of keyword ideas generated by Google. These keywords are taken straight from Google's keyword database, and let's face it, they know what people are searching for, so while the data is not 100% accurate (Google would never want to give us all the facts), they are reliable enough to determine in-demand topics.

The columns you should pay the most attention to are "Avg. Monthly Searches", "Competition" & "Suggested bid".

We want to find phrases that have high average monthly searches, HIGH competition and a high suggested bid.

No, that wasn't a misprint.

No. I meant high competition....

People who look for low competition phrases are the typical web spammers. They want low competition so they can easily rank for the phrase, but why? Probably so they can create a page specifically designed to rank for that phrase (and that is what Google call "Webspam").

A high competition means a lot of advertisers are bidding on the phrase, and if they are bidding on the phrase, it means there is demand. The value of that demand can also be determined by looking at the suggested bid. The higher the bid, the potentially more commercial the term, and therefore from our point of view, if we want to monetize the page in some way, it should be fairly easy to find adverts, or even just use Adsense.

In addition to what I just said, we are not looking to create a page that ranks for that specific term, we are just looking for content ideas. We don't need to worry what phrases we WANT our pages rank for as Google will decide that. I will tell you though that the way we create our pages, will help them rank for dozens, or even hundreds of keyword phrases.

So, look for high Avg. Monthly searches, high competition and high suggest bid. This will identify popular content ideas.

You can order a column from high to low, and low to high by clicking on the column title. Another useful feature of the Keyword Planner is that you can filter your results using the options on the left. Let's say you only want phrases that have a monthly search volume of 5000+, a suggested bid of at least €1 (or maybe $1 in your case, but I am in Europe), and high competition. That would surely weed out a lot of the chaff.

On the left, click on the box titled "Keyword Filters":

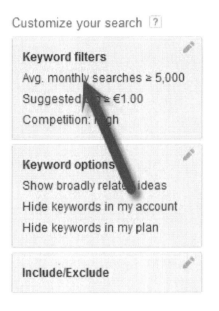

A form opens up, and you can specify your criteria:

Customize your search ?

Average monthly searches ?
≥ ▼   5000

Suggested bid ?
≥ ▼   € 1.00

Ad impression share ?
≥ ▼

Competition
☑ High ☐ Medium ☐ Low

After you make your selection, click away from the filter dialogue (somewhere on the background, like on the table of data). This will close the dialogue and update your results.

Looking down the keywords I've generated and filtered for "weight loss", I can see a few good content ideas:

1. Fast weight loss / Rapid weight loss (always popular in the pre-summer months). Combined, these get around 20,000 searches per month. Note that you can check on seasonality of phrases by putting your mouse over the little graph icon next to the phrase.

Monthly searches for: May 2013 - Apr 2014
Stats also available with downloads

Keyword (by relevance)					
fast weight loss	⬚	12,100	High	€3.00	0%	»
weight loss supplements	⬚	18,100	High	€1.60	0%	»

Notice the higher peaks in March -June.

58

2. Weight loss supplements (though this could be a whole category of content on a weight loss site, with different articles exploring different supplements). We also have weight loss pills related to this search.
3. Weight loss surgery.
4. Diet Plans (again this could be a major category on a weight loss site).
5. Diets that work. This phrase is searched for nearly 15,000 times a month!
6. Medical weight loss is searched for 6,600 times a month, though there will be a lot of related search phrases like gastric surgery, gastric bypass, bariatric surgery, etc.

If you find an area that you would like to look into further, just change the search term at the top of the page. You can enter several words, separated by a comma if you like:

Your product or service

| gastric surgery, gastric bypass, bariatric surgery | Get ideas | Modify search |

You'll get to see the data for those specific phrases:

| Ad group ideas | Keyword ideas | | | 〰 | ↓ Down |

Search terms	Avg. monthly searches [?]	Competition [?]	Suggested bid [?]	Ad imp
gastric bypass	33,100	High	€5.17	
bariatric surgery	49,500	High	€7.11	
gastric surgery	880	High	€9.94	

1 - 3 of 3 keyv

.. as well as all of the related terms generated by the Google keyword tool.

This new set gives me more ideas for content, like:

gastric bypass surgery cost	⌁	1,900	High	€5.15
bariatric surgery diet	⌁	1,300	High	€2.91
what is gastric bypass surgery	⌁	1,000	High	€4.41
gastric bypass complications	⌁	1,300	High	€2.87
what is bariatric surgery	⌁	1,600	High	€6.33
gastric band surgery	⌁	1,000	High	€6.69
weight loss surgery options	⌁	2,900	High	€6.62

Each of these phrases on their own could be the inspiration behind an article, or it would be possible to write about several of these in a single article. It's up to you to decide how you want to handle the keyword data you collect.

Just an important reminder - You WILL NOT be writing an article around any one or more these phrases. These phrases are just the seeds for content ideas. You need to get inside the head of the person typing these phrases into Google and decide why they are typing the phrase?

For example, take that phrase "gastric bypass complications". I'd imagine (though I could be wrong), that the people searching for this phrase are likely to be the potential patients and their families/friends trying to be prepared for all eventualities. In other words, how safe is it? Are complications common?

My initial idea for content might be to find real people who had been through the operation, and interview them about the procedure. With the internet, it is relatively easy to find people who are happy to talk and share experiences.

I'd ask them things like:

- How did the operation go?
- How long was the recovery time?
- What, if anything went wrong?
- How have you found eating since the operation?
- Any words of warning to prospective patients?

- If there was one thing you wished you'd known before the operation, what would it be?

I'd be tempted to find some people that were very happy with the operation and the results, and others that had problems. You could put both sides of the story forward, and offer statistics on how likely someone was to face complications.

That would be an interesting article for my target audience, wouldn't it?

Find phrases that people are looking for, and then try to get into their heads to find out why they are searching for those phrases. Once you can answer that, you can create content that will interest them.

OK, this chapter should have given you lots of ideas on how to find interesting and stimulating content. Remember your main goal. You want to create content that your visitors want to read, and share.

Types of Web Content

.. that will excite your visitors and bring them back looking for more.

With any content that you post on you site, it often helps to think whether or not that content would be something your visitors would want to share with their friends or social media followers. This is a good indicator of the type of quality you should be aiming for.

Ultimately the content on your site will determine whether or not your site succeeds in the long term. Do people bookmark your site? Does your content have a lot of social shares? Does your site offer its visitors a unique experience not found on competing websites?

It doesn't matter if your site is a personal project, an eCommerce site, an affiliate site, or a company website. It MUST offer visitors a reason to return, and that starts with the content on the site. In this chapter, I hope to give you some ideas to get your creative juices flowing. However, before we look at different types of content, I want to talk briefly about link bait.

Link Bait?

Link bait is a term that you may already know. Essentially, link bait is any type of content that was created to attract links back to the page. Link bait tends to be something topical, funny or controversial. It's something that when a visitor sees it, they want to share it with their friends. It's the fact that people want to share it, that makes other webmasters link to the page to share it with their own visitors.

In SEO terms, links to a page are important for ranking purposes, so if we can get other websites to link to our pages, purely because the content is so good, then it's win-win. Increase links, increase traffic AND keep visitors happy with such great content.

Usually when I mention the idea of attracting links naturally by creating great content, I get a number of webmasters suggesting that getting links this way is next to impossible. A lot of webmasters are reluctant to link to other sites, especially if those sites are competitor sites. I'll admit, it's not easy to attract links naturally, but it is something you should aim for. Also, bear in mind that if your content excites your visitors, they WILL share on social media channels, and these channels do create links back to your content. This type of backlink may be weak in terms of SEO rankings, but Google (and other search engines) do monitor social activity, and reward content that gets shared on places like Twitter, Google Plus and Facebook.

From now on, I want you to think about your content in terms of "share bait". I'm not suggesting that you create content specifically to attract links (link bait) or even get shares. I'm suggesting that you create content that your visitors will want to share, and could become link bait because people love it so much. Think of visitor experience first, search engines second.

OK, so let's explore the types of content you can post on your site.

1. Articles

When most webmasters think of content, they think in terms of an article written about a specific topic. This is, of course, a valuable addition to any site as long as the article is well-written, interesting to your target visitor and get's them sharing via social channels.

Thinking of content as "articles" is probably a throwback to the earlier SEO techniques of finding high demand, low competition phrases, and writing a separate piece of content to rank for each phrase. As you know, that is not the type of content you should be creating. If you are going to write a "traditional" article, and there is no reason you should not, you should be trying to make your article unique in terms of content and voice. Are you giving your opinions? Are you adding your own personality? Does the article offer something that is not already out there on competitor websites? Does your article stand out enough that Google will want to show it in the top 10?

For Example: Julie has a website about the Paleo diet and she decides to write an article called "What is the Paleo Diet?" In her article, she wants to talk about what you can and cannot eat while on the Paleo diet.

How is she going to make her article unique, in terms of content and voice, to everything else out there? What is going to stop her article on the dos and don'ts of the Paleo diet from being the same (or very similar) to thousands of other articles on the exact same topic? What is going to make Google take her article above all of the others and put it into the top 10 for a number of related phrases?

OK, I know a lot of you reading this are shouting "LINKS".

Yes, links help content rank. However, it doesn't matter how many links you have to an article if it's not very good. Even if it ranks well initially, the search engines will catch on, and rankings will slide. The first step in getting any piece of content to rank well and STICK in the rankings, is to make that content better than anything else out there, or at least making it different enough (in some interesting way) to warrant a place in the top 10.

To make her article on "What is the Paleo Diet?" different, she could write an article on the things she found most difficult about adapting to the Paleo diet. What food items SHE misses, and how she's replaced them with Paleo-friendly alternatives. In other words, she could write it from a personal standpoint and inject her own personality into the article.

An example might be that she found it very difficult to give up bread and cakes. She could then link to recipes on her site offering paleo bread and paleo cake recipes. She might also miss peanut butter (peanuts are legumes and they aren't allowed), but she has a great almond butter recipe that totally makes up for it.

After writing the article, she might decide that her title of "What is the Paleo Diet?" is a little too generic and rename it something like "My favourite Paleo-friendly alternatives to old food addictions."

OK, that title is just off the top of my head, but it's a good starting point, and I can see that type of article being "share bait" in the Paleo community.

In the days of yore, webmasters would have laughed at me for suggesting a title that did not contain a keyword phrase, but you know better, don't you?

My point should be clear. Your articles need to stand out and offer visitors something that is not already in the top 10, otherwise why would Google consider ranking your article above the current top 10? You articles need to be interesting enough to encourage your readers to share it through social channels. It's through social sharing that other people (and search engines) will start to take notice.

A lot of the types of content we'll look at in this chapter are "articles" in the traditional sense. However, looking at them as different categories or types of article is helpful, because it can stimulate new ideas and opportunities for entertaining our visitors. Let's get on.

2. PDF

PDF stands for portable document format, and is a standard way to distribute a document of some sort. I like to create at least one PDF document for a website because of its versatility.

Ways you can use a PDF include:

- Offer it as an incentive to sign up for a newsletter.
- Distribute it to a number of document sharing sites, which not only get more eyes on the document, but also offer an opportunity to get a link back to your site.
- Add affiliate links to the document, and give it away. When a reader clicks through on an affiliate link, and makes a purchase, you make a commission. For example, if you had a "juicing" site, you could create a PDF that reviews the top juicers, link to the juicers via affiliate links, and give the report away.
- Create a PDF eBook and sell it on your site.

PDFs can be downloaded and read on computers and mobile devices, so offer your visitors another way to digest your content.

3. Images including mind maps, infographics, diagrams etc

Don't underestimate the value of quality diagrams. They can be flow charts, mind maps, or simple diagrams used to explain a point in your text. You have heard the phrase a picture is worth a thousand words? Well, that applies to a web page too, and great images tend to be shared more than most other types of content, especially since Pinterest and other image sharing sites arrived on the scenes.

If a diagram can help you explain something, use one.

There are some great graphics packages available for creating diagrams. My personal favourite is called eDraw Max. It allows users to create a wide range of diagrams, including mind maps, infographics, flow charts, etc. You can read a review I wrote of the tool here:

http://ezseonews.com/review/diagrams-mind-maps-more/

A popular free graphics tool is the Gimp:

http://www.gimp.org/

Be warned though, it comes with quite a learning curve.

4. Video

Google own Youtube and probably because of that, you see a lot of Youtube videos ranking in the top 10 of Google for a wide range of search terms.

You can create a Youtube channel free of charge. If you create a video and upload it to your channel, you can embed that video into a web page on your site.

Good videos get shared a lot on social media.

Again, Google own Youtube, so know when a video is popular, and they can make good videos rank highly in the SERPs.

Creating a video does not need to be expensive or complicated. You could record yourself or someone else on your Smartphone and upload the video to your Youtube channel. Alternatively you could record your computer screen to create tutorials using freely available tools like Camstudio (http://camstudio.org/), not to be confused with Camtasia Studio which is quite expensive. Another popular free tool is Screencast-O-Matic (http://www.screencast-o-matic.com/).

Create a video, upload it to Youtube and embed it on a page as part of a larger article.

Good videos also increase the time a visitor stays on your site. Since time on site is something that Google monitors, this can only be good for your SEO efforts.

5. FAQs

By their very name, FAQs or "frequently asked questions" are exactly the type of content you should be including on your website. After all, they are the common questions that real visitors ask.

Whenever you get an email from a visitor asking a question, create a webpage on your site that displays the question and your answer. You can then send that person the webpage (containing social sharing buttons).

This not only makes them aware of your site, if they weren't already, but it adds valuable content to your site, and keeps the person who asked the question happy. If you include their name as part of the question, they might even share the webpage with their friends. Everyone wants five minutes of fame!

Over time, a FAQ section on your site will grow, offering a really valuable resource to your visitors.

6. Photos

Note that you cannot just download and use any photo you want on your website. If you find a photo that you want to use, you must check out the licensing for that photo. There are also stock photo sites where you can buy a license to use photos.

OK, with that said, how can you use photos on your site?

People don't generally like reading large blocks of text. If you can split it up with interesting photos, it makes the content easier to digest. They don't need to be professional quality photos. In fact, using your mobile phone to take the photos can add to the charm of your web pages, since a visitor can see that there is a real person behind the site.

Another excellent use of photos is as a type of "link bait". People love funny photos, photos of animals or babies and just anything that makes them laugh or go "ahhhh".

Depending on the type of site you run, you might be able to think of photos that people would want to share. With photo sharing sites like Pinterest, Flickr, Shutterfly and Instagram, photos can really help boost traffic (and links) to your site.

So you want a few examples?

If you ran a juicing site, cute pictures of babies spilling juice all over themselves would be fun, though be careful not to abuse your own child if you take these photos yourself ☺.

If you ran a pet site, the possible photo opportunities are endless, from cute puppies, to the photo of your Rottweiler snuggling up to your pet rat or budgie.

If you ran a skin care website, maybe you could show photos of the "worst tan ever". Just Google it and you'll see what I mean. You could even run a competition on your site for "worst tan" photo submissions.

If you want to see how photos have been used by others, go to Google and just search for viral photos. You'll find some really great ones.

There is also nothing to stop you taking a photo and adding text to the photo, to make it funny. I'm sure you have seen these all over the internet.

7. Sounds files

With more and more people using smart phones, sound files in various forms have become very popular. You have probably heard of audiobooks and podcasts. These are two different forms of sound files that people can download and listen to as they drive to work, go to the gym, or stroll through the countryside with their dog.

Not everyone has the time to create a regular podcast, but a series of downloadable audio files could be created in one go, and released over time, maybe as part of an autoresponder. The audio can be saved as MP3 files, which makes them instantly useable by just about every mobile device out there.

If you do have the time for a regular podcast, this is one of the very best ways to build your audience. You can submit the podcast to various podcast directories, like iTunes, and as long as you create interesting audio, you will grow an audience of people who feel a real connection to you. After all, they are listening to you in the comfort of their own home, or car, and it's a regular "meeting".

What can you talk about? Well that depends on your niche, but I would certainly reference content on your site, so that listeners will be interested enough to go and visit your website for more details.

8. How stuff works

I like this type of content. People are always looking for tutorials online to learn new skills. Tutorials can be text based, with lots of screen captures, or video based. We mentioned video earlier in this chapter, so go back and check for free screen capture software where you can record your computer screen. Alternatively you could just record tutorials, or "lessons", on your mobile phone and upload them to a site like Youtube. Youtube can host all of your video content, which is a big money-saver for you. If you want to create videos that do not appear in the Youtube search, you can create private videos. The only way to find private videos is via a link that you can share with select people.

Personally, I like a mixture of good video tutorials with a text based version (with lots of screenshots) as well. I have found that some people prefer to watch, while others prefer to read and follow along.

9. Top 10 lists

Top 10 lists are often found on sites like Stumbleupon, where users share content that they find interesting. Stumbleupon content can very easily go viral as users vote content up or down. If your content gets a positive response, your site could end up getting a lot of attention.

Look at this:

I searched Google for pages on the Stumbleupon website that include the phrase "top 10" on the page.

The search string consists of two parts:

1. Site:stumbleupon.com – this tells Google to only return pages that are on the StumbleUpon domain.
2. "top 10" – which tells Google that all pages must include the phrase "top 10"

Google report that there are currently over 1 million matches, but that is a little misleading, because if we narrow the search to only include top 10 articles on Stumbleupon that include the word "juice", then we get this:

Hmmm. Nearly 3 million matches.

So what type of top 10 lists can you create?

Anything that you think your visitor will be interested in.

- Top 10 reasons diets fail
- Top 10 celebrities on the Atkins diet
- Top 10 Wordpress plugins
- Top 10 reasons your car will fail this year
- Top 10 reasons to eat more spinach
- Top 10 reasons baby cry
- Top 10 things women like to hear
- Top 10 things men like to hear

Simply identify a problem and offer the top 10 causes or ways to solve that problem.

As you can see, it's easy to come up with ideas for just about any niche.

If you struggle to come up with your own ideas, you can search Google for existing top 10 articles in your niche, and borrow ideas from what you find. For example, I run a juicing site so this might work:

site:stumbleupon.com "top 10" intitle:juice

Web   Images   Videos   Shopping   News   More ▾   Search tools

About 1,050 results (0.18 seconds)

Top 10 juice fast recipes for alcohol abuse and liver detox ...
www.stumbleupon.com/su/19Y6ap ▾ StumbleUpon ▾
Login. Sign Up. Share this page: **Top 10** juice fast recipes for alcohol abuse and liver detox. Friday May 23rd 2014. Facebook. Twitter. Google. YouTube. Rss.

Chart **Juice**: Rihanna, Usher Roar Into **Top 10** - StumbleUpon
www.stumbleupon.com/...**juice**/chart-**juice**-rihanna-usher-roar... StumbleUpon ▾
Billboard. Videos. Photos. Articles. Artists. Search form. Hot 100. Billboard 200. Genres. International. All Charts. Podcast. Chart Juice: Rihanna, Usher Roar Into ...

Top 10 Aloe Vera **Juice** Benefits - StumbleUpon
www.stumbleupon.com/.../**top-10**-aloe-vera-**juice**-benefits/ ▾ StumbleUpon ▾
Share this page: **Top 10** Aloe Vera Juice Benefits. **Top 10** Aloe Vera Juice Benefits. Home > Herbal Remedies > Aloe Vera. Aloe vera juice benefits make this ...

In this search string, I used another variable:

Intitle:juice

This tells Google to only return pages that have the word juice in the web page title. I included it because I only wanted articles that are about juicing, and not those that might just mention the word "juice" in a sidebar or similar.

That search returned over 1000 top 10 articles on Stumbleupon that include the word "juice" in the title.   There should be plenty of ideas there, although not all will be about the type of juice I am looking for.

If I was doing this exercise to find ideas, I would also use "juicing" as a search term to narrow the results.

To make it easy for visitors to share your content on sites like Stumbleupon, include social share icons on your web pages including the one for Stumbleupon:

See the social sharing button chapter in this book for more details.

10.   Resources

Resources can be anything that your visitors might find interesting.

It might lists of articles on other web sites, relevant web forums, computer software, interesting images, etc.

You could have a resource page which links out to your recommended resources, or you might decide to have a resource box at the end of an article, with a few resources relevant to that article.   The idea is simply to offer your visitors more value, by highlighting resources you think they will be interested in.

If you are linking out to other websites, I do recommend you open those links in a new window so you don't lose the visitor from your own site.

11.   "Recipes"

Recipes?

Think of "recipes for a happy marriage", or "recipes for a stress free life".

There is also the type of recipe you use in a kitchen, so let's look at those first.

This one depends very much on the type of site you have, but recipes are a great way to get people coming back to your website. If you have any type of health site, lots of generic recipes are relevant. If you have a health site focusing on a specific problem, e.g. fat loss, diabetes, etc., you can include recipes specific to your niche (recipes to help with fat loss, or sugar-free recipes for diabetics).

Even if you don't have a health site, think outside the box a little. For example, if you run a "computer" site, maybe a "recipe for a virus free computer" (recommendations for anti-virus, anti-spyware, firewall etc as a kind of recipe).

If you have a motoring website, maybe "a recipe for trouble free motoring" (check the oil, water levels, tyre pressure etc before a long trip), or even a more literal recipe for a window cleaner you make yourself from kitchen ingredients.

The point is not necessarily using the word "recipe" in the article or even thinking in terms of a traditional recipe. This is more of a mental crutch to help you think of interesting things your visitors will appreciate and make their lives easier.

Recipe type content like this, is great share-bait.

Writing Styles

Something you might like to think about is the style of the article you are writing.

While articles should always be informative, they can be written in a number of different styles.

The 2 main styles I usually think of are:

- Journalist / Facts – where you try to be as impartial as possible, giving the information in an interesting way. Think about writing an article for a newspaper.
- Story telling & personal - Visitors love reading real stories about, and written by, real people.

You may find that 100% of your content is a mixture of the two, which we could classify as a third style:

- A combination of facts and personal – where you provide the facts like a journalist would, but offer your own thoughts, theories, experiences, etc, into the mix.

An example of a personal story telling style might start like this:

"Today I feel great thanks to the Atkins diet, but it wasn't always that way. Just 12 months ago, 50lbs over-weight and with blood pressure running to 160/100, I had to get in shape. The Atkins diet appealed to me because I was allowed to eat lots of meat, and hunger wasn't a problem on the diet. However, before embarking on the diet, I needed to find out if it was safe"...

This method tells the reader that you have been through their situation and can offer valuable help based on your real-life experience. They want to know how the Atkins diet worked out for you, and are more likely to trust you having read your personal story and know that you went through it.

I would limit this type of article to those topics where you have actually experienced what you are writing about. Of course, if you want to write that type of article but have not gone through the experience, you could always "interview" people who have been through it and offer their experiences in your article. This article might start off in a very similar way:

"I'm 50lbs over-weight and my blood pressure is 160/100. I really need to get in shape. The Atkins diet appeals to me because I can eat lots of meat, so hunger won't be a problem like the calorie-controlled diets I have tried in the past. However, before I start the diet, I need to know it's safe."...

This article could go on:

"Luckily I found 3 people who have been on the diet, and have had the chance to chat with them about their experiences on the diet, their results and more importantly their blood work analysis before and after the diet."....

Here is another example of the personal style article:

"My sister has battled the bulge all her adult life. At 50 pounds over-weight, the final straw was when her doctor used the words 'morbidly obese'".

This article is based on the experiences of someone close to you, so is still very personal, and that will come through as you tell the story.

If the person was not known personally to you, but you interviewed or chatted with them to get their story (moving into journalistic style now), then the article might start off like this:

e.g. "Peter was 40 years old and 100 lb overweight. His doctor told him that he was morbidly obese, and needed to lose weight to avoid health complications. I was lucky enough to chat with him..."

In this article, we might get a combination of the personal and journalistic styles, as you add in your own thoughts, personal experiences or advice.

Of course, if you want to keep your own thoughts and opinions out of the article, and simply report the facts, articles can become more like the pieces you would read in a newspaper.

This may be the style you prefer to use when you write about topics you don't have personal experience with, and can't find third-party stories to base your article on.

e.g. "The Atkins diet is based on high protein, low fat meals, and has been responsible for massive weight loss in a number of prominent celebrities. However, health concerns often arise whenever the Atkins diet is reviewed.....", and so on.

I don't want you to think that you have to decide on a style and stick to it. Usually the style comes out as you write, and you should be flexible in your content writing. I **suggest you think of style more as an idea generator**. This has always helped me come up with a lot of different ideas and approaches for a particular topic I want to cover.

75

Ask yourself:

"What personal stories can I write about weight loss?"

"If I was a newspaper journalist, what angles can I come up with to write an article that isn't the same as every other weight loss article?"

Starting with these two questions, you should be able to come up with a number of ideas, and then settle on the best one for the article. If that article ends up mixing journalist and personal approach, then so be it. As long as it entertains and informs your visitors, then you have succeeded in your mission.

Pretty much any type of article you create for your site will fit one of these two main styles, or be a mixture of the two. Go back and look at the chapter on "Types of Content", and think how each of the examples I gave could be written in a journalistic style, and in a personal style.

Examples:

- A product review can come alive if written from personal experience (which it should be). However, a certain degree of journalism will add much needed information about the product you are reviewing. Adding in the views of other people you have spoken to will add more value to your review.
- A Q&A session might by mainly journalistic, but adding in your own personal thoughts and experiences can bring the Q&A to life.
- You might have a page of facts, maybe a top 10 list. That may well be just a journalistic piece, but you could add in some personal insights too.
- Think how you would write a tutorial for something. It's mainly about writing facts in a way that helps the visitor understand how to do something, but it is also useful to add in your own experiences, tips and tricks.

OK, let's look at something I call "Niche Vocabulary", because all good text based content has it.

Niche Vocabulary

If you had two articles in front of you, one written by an expert, the other not, you could tell them apart, right?

Google certainly seem to be able to as well.

How is it that Google can analyze documents and spot those that are written by experts? And remember, for the most part it is computer code that is doing the analyzing for Google, not humans.

There are a number of tell-tale signs that a computer can easily pick up.

Think about spelling and grammar. Word processors do a reasonable job at this, so you'd expect Google to be able to as well.

Grammatical and spelling errors often appear in poorly written or rushed work. However, they can just as easily appear in articles written by experts. If an article is not proofed before it is uploaded, even the most authoritative articles could have spelling or grammatical errors.

While Google do take notice of spelling and grammar, and can penalize for it, I don't think it is a major ranking factor unless it is clear that spelling mistakes were included on the page deliberately to help a page rank for misspelled search phrases.

One thing that is common to all quality articles is the "language" they use. For every topic, there are words and phrases that MUST appear in that article because those words and phrases are ESSENTIAL to that topic.

For example, if I was writing an article on diabetes, I really would have to use words like:

Diabetes, insulin, glucose, blood, type, levels, sugar and so on.

Any expert writing an article on diabetes would include these (and other essential) words NATURALLY as they wrote. This is the "language" I referred to earlier. Every article you write will have its own "niche vocabulary" that will ultimately help Google decide what the article is about and rank accordingly.

Let's take the above example of diabetes a step further.

There are different types of diabetes – type 1 diabetes and type 2 diabetes. If you had 2 articles, one on each and both written by an expert, would the niche vocabulary be the same?

The answer is some of it.

For example, both articles would probably include those keywords we listed earlier:

Diabetes, insulin, glucose, blood, type, levels, sugar

However, each article would also include words or phrases that were a little more specific to that type of diabetes.

The type 1 diabetes article might include: autoimmune, pancreas, stops producing insulin, beta cells, genetic factor

The type 2 diabetes article might include: lifestyle, diet, insulin resistance, non-insulin dependent, adult-onset, obesity

The niche vocabulary would have some overlap, but overall they are quite distinct.

Niche vocabulary for type 1 & type 2 diabetes

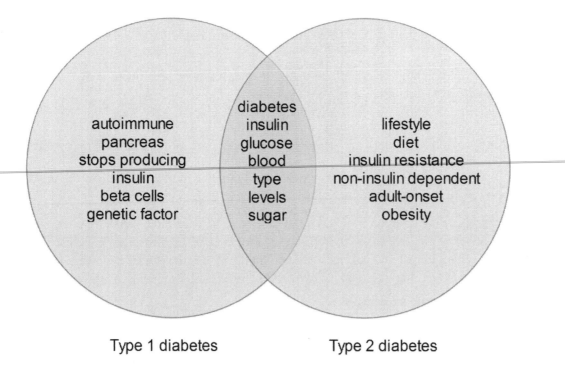

Type 1 diabetes   Type 2 diabetes

We could take this even further if we include a type of type 2 diabetes known as gestational diabetes:

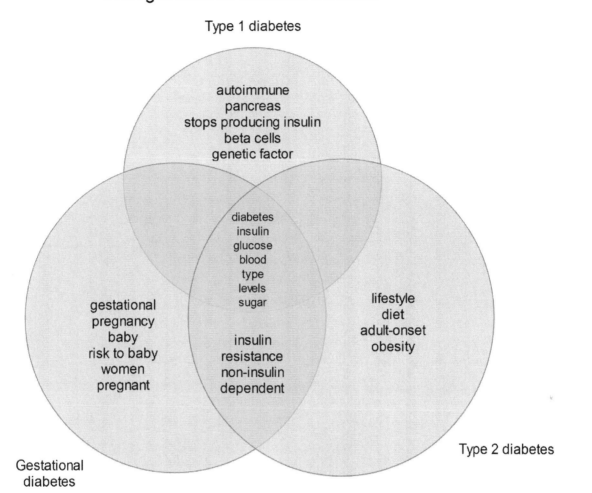

With gestational diabetes included

Type 1 diabetes

autoimmune
pancreas
stops producing insulin
beta cells
genetic factor

diabetes
insulin
glucose
blood
type
levels
sugar

insulin
resistance
non-insulin
dependent

gestational
pregnancy
baby
risk to baby
women
pregnant

lifestyle
diet
adult-onset
obesity

Type 2 diabetes

Gestational
diabetes

The diagram isn't entirely correct above, as some words or phrases may appear in other areas, but as an illustration, I think you can see that different topics have their own, unique vocabulary. Where similar topics overlap, you see similar niche vocabulary in those topics.

It would be IMPOSSIBLE to write a great article on gestational diabetes without using most, if not all of those words and phrases in the Gestational diabetes circle above, wouldn't it?

Every article or piece of content will have its own unique list of words and phrases that are important to that article.

From Google's point of view, looking for sets (or groups) of words and phrases on a page will help them understand what the page is about, and make it easier for them to match the pages in their index to the searchers request. It also allows them to find the better articles on a topic, because they know that those better articles will have the correct niche vocabulary.

A quick look at Google Search

If I go to Google and type in "Lost", Google don't really know what I am looking for:

Am I searching for information on a lost plane? Lost girl? The Lost in Space series?

As soon as I add another word, Google can start looking for known sets:

Apologies to anyone that isn't a "Lost" (as in the TV Series) fan. Google immediately associated the words "Lost" and "Freckles" and is now pretty sure what I am looking for, since most of the suggestions refer to the Lost TV series. Google also knows that "Sawyer" is relevant to this search term.

They aren't 100% sure as I might be looking for information on losing freckles!

By the way, for non-fans, Freckles is the nickname given to Evangeline Lilly's character by "Sawyer", the character played by Josh Holloway. Google know this, and offer me suggestions to help me refine my "Lost" search.

Depending on what I choose from the list of alternatives, Google will have a better idea of exactly what I am looking for, and be able to serve up the most relevant search results.

For example, if I click on "lost freckles sawyer", I am probably going to get more search results that include references to Josh and the character he plays. If, however, I choose "freckles lost actress", I'd expect to see more pages in the SERPs relating to Evangeline Lilly and her character. Think how the niche vocabulary would be different in both of those sets of articles.

Google try to understand exactly what you want, then look for documents in their database that have the correct niche vocabulary for that particular search term.

Incidentally, these search suggestions are based on search queries entered at Google. The ones at the top of the list are the more common ones, so this is another interesting way to find content ideas.

How can we use this information?

It might be that you want to rank a page for "lost freckles sawyer". The old way of doing that would be to create a page, with:

- Lost-freckles-sawyer as the filename.
- Lost freckles sawyer in the title.
- Lost freckles sawyer in an H1 header.
- Lost freckles sawyer in the opening paragraph and sprinkled throughout the article.
- Lost freckles sawyer in a hyperlink somewhere.
- Lost freckles sawyer as the name of an image.
- .. and so on...

The problem is, the phrase "Lost freckles sawyer" does not make sense. Any page created as shown above would clearly be bad quality, and something Google would call "Webspam".

However, pages created like this used to rank well, even a few short years ago. This was how many webmasters created their content!

You may even still find content in Google that looks as if it was written around a keyword phrase like this, but it is becoming rarer, and Google will stamp on it when they find it, often de-indexing the offending site.

So, how exactly do you rank for "lost freckles sawyer" if you cannot have that exact phrase on the page?

Simple.

Find out what someone is really looking for when they type that search phrase into Google (searcher intent), and then work out the niche vocabulary.

It's not as difficult as you might think. Pages in Google rank for that term, so all you need to do is study the top 10. What "niche vocabulary" are they using which is helping them rank for that phrase? What words and phrases are essential to write a good article on the searcher intent?

Finding Theme Words & Phrases

There are a number of tools that can help you find good sets of theme words and phrases for any topic you want to write about. Some are free, some are not. I'll show you the best free way and the best paid tool for the job.

Free Option 1 – Google SERPs

Simply go to Google, search for the phrase you want to rank for, and look through the top 10 results ranking for that term. As you read through those top 10 pages, make a note of any niche vocabulary that you see.

This can be a time-consuming method for finding the niche vocabulary for a topic (but I will show you a free tool you can use to speed it up). This method does have the added bonus of showing you the pages that actually rank for a phrase, which in itself is a great way to spark ideas for content.

As you look through the pages:

- Note down anything that looks interesting or unique to specific web pages.
- What are the sub-headings found in the top ranked pages?
- Are there any cool features of the content that really make the pages stand out?
- What features of these top 10 pages make them deserve to be in the top 10?

OK, I told you a minute ago that there was a free tool to help speed up the collection of niche vocabulary. In fact, it's a web browser add-on called SEOQuake. It's available for Chrome, Firefox, Opera and Safari:

http://www.seoquake.com/

I personally use Google Chrome, so I'll show you how to use the add-on in Chrome. It will be very similar in the other browsers.

Once installed, SEOQuake adds a button to the right of you address bar:

It should be easy to spot, as it has an "S" and a "Q" in the button. It will be disabled by default, and in fact we don't need to enable it to use the feature I want to show you.

Do a Google search for something of interest, and visit one of the pages in the top 10. I did a search for "Lost freckles sawyer" and pulled up this wikia page:

http://lostpedia.wikia.com/wiki/Skate

OK, now click on the SEOQuake button, and select "Page Info":

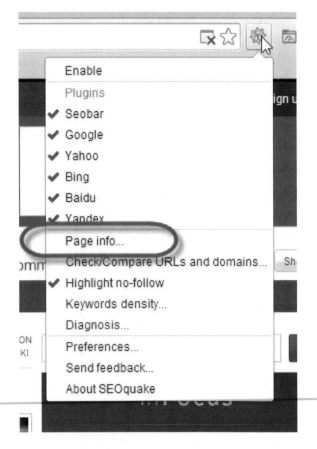

A new tab in the browser opens showing you information about the page, including "keyword density", which is pure gold for mining niche vocabulary:

Keywords density:

Total number of words: 5237

Keyword	Found in	Repeats	Density
sawyer	D	214	4.09%
kate	D	205	3.91%
day		43	0.82%
jack		39	0.74%
juliet		27	0.52%
island		27	0.52%
later		22	0.42%

Scroll down further and you'll find 2 word phrases:

Total 2 word phrases: 392

Keyword	Found in	Repeats	Density
- day		40	1.53%
sawyer and	D	36	1.37%
and kate	D	33	1.26%
kate and		21	0.80%
and sawyer		20	0.76%
the island		19	0.73%
sawyer s		16	0.61%
kate s	D	13	0.50%
days ago		11	0.42%

.. and 3 word phrases:

Total 3 word phrases: 200

Keyword	Found in	Repeats	Density
sawyer and kate	D	26	1.49%
kate and sawyer		12	0.69%
by wholocked11 16		8	0.46%
16 days ago		8	0.46%
wholocked11 16 days		8	0.46%
part 1 -		7	0.40%
in the flash-sideways		7	0.40%
he doesn t		6	0.34%

You may also have 4-word phrases on longer pages.

The 2, 3 and 4-word phrases often have a lot more irrelevant stuff, since the tool isn't finding actual "phrases", but 2, 3 & 4 word sequences of words. However, this is still useful, it just takes a little more time to sort through the 2, 3 & 4 word phrases.

The density in the final column tells you how many times each word or phrase appeared on the page, so the more a phrase appears, the more likely it is to be important.

By looking at the information on this page, I can put together a simple niche vocabulary for an article on this topic in about 5 minutes:

Sawyer, kate, jack, Juliet, season, lost, gun, pickett, relationship, escape, freckles, feelings, kiss, fight, hurley, ben, Malcolm David Kelley, water, leaves, survivors, threatens, found, airport, the island, flash-sideways, the beach, the jungle, polar bear, the temple

I only just started watching Lost this month, and am only part way through season 1, so I do recognize the relevance of most of these words, however, there are some I do not recognize, and that is the beauty of using tools to find niche vocabulary. Even if you do not know a topic, you can still find out the important words and phrases you should be using, even if you then have to research how they are to be used.

For example, in the words above there are some names of people. I recognize Hurley, but cannot place Pickett, Juliet, Ben or Malcom David Kelley (I am really bad with actor's names). I do know that these names are important though, so a quick check of the original webpage, or Google, and I can find out who they are and how they fit into the content.

By going through a few of the top 10 pages, you can quickly build up a niche vocabulary for any topic you want to write about.

This will then serve you as a blueprint for your own article.

Free Option 2 - LSI Keywords

LSIKeywords.com is a free online tool for finding theme words and phrases. You essentially enter a keyword phrase, and LSIKeywords goes off to analyze the top 5 or so pages in Google and returns a list of theme words and phrases (i.e. niche vocabulary).

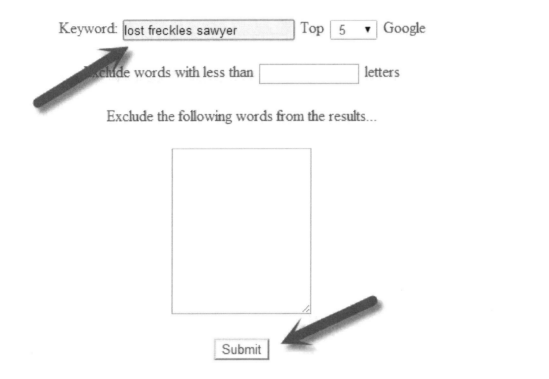

When it works, it does a pretty thorough job and I definitely recommend you test it out.

I only have two reservations about this tool.

1. LSI Keywords will tell you how many times a word or phrase appears in total on the top 5 (or more) pages in the SERPs, but that isn't a true reflection of how important a keyword is. A keyword may only appear on one of the top 5 pages, which when you think about it means it's not that important (important niche vocabulary will appear on most, if not all of the top 5-10 pages). However, if that keyword appears 50 times on that one page, you might be misled into thinking it was important.

2. LSIKeywords often throws up an error and won't give you anything useful. At the time of writing this section of the book, I searched for "lost freckles sawyer" and got an error message:

Error Net::HTTPFound

Clearly this will be quite frustrating if you are trying to do research for a piece of content, but remember, this is a free tool using lots of resources, so just having it as an option is a good thing.

Paid Option - Web Content Studio

Firstly I want to add a disclaimer.

I created and own Web Content Studio (WCS), so the following discussion is about my own tool, and obviously if you buy, I am the one receiving your money.

While I feel that WCS is the best paid tool for web content writers, I do not want this book to be seen as a sale pitch for my own tool. I therefore won't go into a lot of detail here, but will instead, state the main benefits of the tool, and send you to a web page where you can see me writing an article with it.

Benefits of WCS

The main benefits of using WCS are:

1. The speed of finding niche vocabulary.
2. WCS will tell you which are the more important words and phrases (i.e. the ones that appear on most of the top 10 pages).
3. The WYSIWYG article editor and theme reports tell you how good a job you've done.

Let's look at those benefits.

Using SEOQuake to find the niche vocabulary is great, but it is slow. You need to go to several pages in the top 10 and analyze each one in turn. You then need to collate all of the results into a single "spreadsheet", showing which terms were the most important across several of the top ranking pages.

The first major benefit of Web Content Studio (WCS) is that you enter a keyword phrase into the "Spider", and WCS goes off and visits the top 10 pages (or however many you like) for you, bringing back the theme words and phrases on all 10 pages.

It then presents a single table of ALL theme words and phrases across all 10 pages.

Once you have chosen the words and phrases that you want to use, WCS will go back and analyze those words and phrases for you to determine how many of the top 10 pages the keyword appears on. If a word or phrase only appears on one or two of the top 10 pages, then it probably is not very important, is it? If, however, a word or phrase appears on 8, 9 or 10 of the top 10 pages, it's much more likely to be an important part of the niche vocabulary.

Another major benefit of WCS is that there is a built in WYSIWYG editor to write your content. When you finish your first draft, you can get WCS to analyze the content against the niche vocabulary it collected in the previous step. Any words or phrases not found in your content can be quickly spotted, as well as any word or phrase that may have been used a few too many times.

There are a lot of other features of this tool that you might find useful, but as I said, I don't want this to sound like a sales pitch. I'll leave you to investigate further if you are interested. Besides, I would highly recommend you to use the free option for harvesting niche vocabulary first.

To see me using the WCS to write an article, visit this page:

http://ezseonews.com/writing-content/how-i-write-a-top-quality-article/

For more details on the tool itself, visit:

http://webcontentstudio.com

OK, we know how to find the niche vocabulary for any piece of content we want to create. But before we look at the actual writing and anatomy of a good piece of web content, I bet you'd like some proof that what I am saying about niche vocabulary is real?

Proof that top pages use "Niche Vocabulary"

Several years ago when I started writing about the need to "theme" content, not everyone believed me. To help prove my point, I created a tool that could not only find niche vocabulary for any topic, but it could take that niche vocabulary, and analyze as many of the Google search results as I wanted.

My research was a few simple steps:

1. Pick a search term.
2. Find the niche vocabulary for that search term by analyzing the pages that ranked for that term.
3. Analyze pages in Google (ranking at various points, like top 10, position 100-110, position 200-210, etc) to see what percentage of the niche vocabulary they were using.

If niche vocabulary was real, and Google preferred pages that contained the niche vocabulary, then I figured that ALL pages in the main Google index would contain a high percentage of the niche vocabulary. Those that didn't SHOULD be consigned to the Supplemental index as "inferior" pages that didn't offer enough value.

Let me take you through an example that we used earlier in the book – gestational diabetes. I've deliberately picked a competitive term to make sure that Google has several hundred high quality results for this search query.

Using WCS I found the following niche vocabulary for the term "gestational diabetes":

diabetes, men, gestational, pregnancy, glucose, blood, eat, health, test, baby, risk, level, women, age, insulin, levels, high, low, type, during, sugar, develop, screening, healthy, help, weight, birth, pregnant, control, normal, doctor, diet, body, signs, food, tolerance, information, factors, increased, condition, tests, check, eating, problems, symptoms, developing, family, treatment, diagnosis, delivery, complications, diagnosed, medical, safe, medicine, exercise, heart, disease, history, mothers, babies, conditions, prevention, skin, nutrition, doctors

The tool also found the following 2, 3 and 4 word phrases:

weeks 24 and 28, after pregnancy, before you get pregnant, blood glucose tests, cause problems, control your blood glucose, delay type 2 diabetes, developing type 2 diabetes, develops only during pregnancy, diabetes medicine, diabetic diet, diagnosis of gestational diabetes, early pregnancy, glucose for energy, glucose testing, glucose tests, high blood glucose levels, high blood sugar levels, higher chance, how to treat, obstetrics and gynecology, oral glucose tolerance test, polycystic ovarian syndrome,

90

prevalence of gestational diabetes, respiratory distress, respiratory distress syndrome, risk factors, risk of gestational diabetes, screening glucose challenge test, screening tests, starchy vegetables, tested for gestational diabetes, treat gestational diabetes, what is gestational diabetes, women with gestational diabetes, yeast infection

That's a lot of theme phrases, but I am not suggesting you try to incorporate all or even most of these phrases in an article. These really become useful in helping plan out the article, giving you pointers on what you should cover. Typically an article might only include 4 or 5 of them.

For the theme analysis, I am more interested in the single words we identified, and the words that make up the phrases.

If you look at those words and phrase, you can see how a good quality article on gestational diabetes must include a large proportion of them.

My next step in the experiment is to find the URLs that rank for the term "gestational diabetes" in Google. I use a tool called Scrapebox to grab all the URLs that rank for the term.

Scrapebox returned only a few hundred URLs ranking for this term. Can that be right? If I search Google for gestational diabetes, Google tells me:

gestational diabetes	🎤	🔍

Web   Books   Images   News   Videos   More ▾   Search tools

About 7,790,000 results (0.47 seconds)

Wow, there should be nearly 8 million URLs ranking for this term, shouldn't there?

Well, Google only actually ever shows a maximum of 1000 URLs, and all the rest are pushed into the Supplemental results. If I scroll to the end of the Google results for this search, I can see this:

‹ Goooogle

Previous   1   2   3   **4**

That means Google only actually rate 387 pages in response to this query. The other 7.8 million are all in supplemental!

OK, so next step is to import the ranking URLs into my tool, together with the niche vocabulary found using WCS.

My first analysis is to look at those pages ranking in the following areas:

1-10, 11-20, 21-30, 31-40, 41-50, 51-60 & 61-70.

Here is the table of results the tool returned:

Position	Theme Score		% Theme Words Used	
1 - 10 (10)	94.9%	5	76.5 %	41
10 - 19 (10)	89.7%		70.2 %	4
20 - 29 (9)	93.2%		61.1 %	216
30 - 39 (10)	92.9%	75	75.5 %	32
40 - 49 (10)	93.2%	72	74.5 %	57
50 - 59 (10)	90%	6	68.2 %	3
60 - 69 (9)	99.6%	7	71.7 %	58

The first column tells you where the web pages that were analyzed came from in the SERPs. The number in brackets indicates how many of the pages in that group were analyzed. If it is less than 10, the reason is simply that a page could not ne loaded during the analysis. One other thing to point out is that there is an error in my labeling of the position. The correct positions are listed above the screenshot, and run from 1-10, 11-20 and so on. Since this analysis tool is only for my own use, I have never fixed this.

The second column is the average theme score for the pages in that group. This uses the same calculation as WCS to determine how well articles are themed. The closer to 100% the more themed an article (comparing it to the selected niche vocabulary).

The third column is the average percentage of the theme words found in the articles.

As you can see, all of the pages ranking in the top 70 of Google have a good percentage of the niche vocabulary. When you consider that the niche vocabulary contains 66 theme words in total, that's quite impressive.

However, what would happen if we analyzed pages further down in Google?

Let's run that experiment as well. Here we look at the pages ranking at positions 1-10, 100-110, 200-210 and 300-310. You might expect those pages that rank near the end of the search results (remember there are only 387 of them) to contain a lot less niche vocabulary?

Here are the results:

Position	Theme Score		% Theme Words Used	
1 - 10 (10)	94.9%	55	76.5 %	
100 - 109 (10)	100%	7	65.5 %	3
200 - 209 (10)	92.3%	56	58.3 %	2
300 - 309 (10)	94.9%	8	67.9 %	
-	-		-	
-	-		-	

The important column to keep your eye on is the last one. This shows the average percentage of niche vocabulary found on the webpages ranking in those position ranges.

Pages ranking in the top 10 used 76% of the theme words.

Pages ranking 100-110 used 65% of the theme words

Pages ranking 200-210 used 58% of the theme words.

Pages ranking 300-310 used 68% of the theme words.

In other words, on average, all of the 387 pages that currently rank for the term gestational diabetes contain a high percentage of niche vocabulary.

It shouldn't really be a surprise, since that niche vocabulary is essential to writing a good article on the topic. Any article that did not contain a good percentage has no right to be ranking in the first place.

All of this goes to show that Google are actually doing a pretty good job. It also goes to show that you need to be thinking in terms of niche vocabulary if you don't want to be consigned to the Supplemental Index.

Writing content that contains theme words and phrases is a very important part of creating web pages that can rank and stick in Google. However, in the next section, we'll look at a number of other factors that you need to be thinking about.

Let's Write!

In the previous sections we looked at finding the niche vocabulary for any piece of content we want to create.

Thoughts on the Actual Content

In this section, I want to take you through a "checklist" of things to consider as you write your content, and create your web page.

Checkpoint #1 - How will your content be better?

If you've been through the manual process of collecting niche vocabulary for your content, then you will have already visited some of the top 10 pages you are competing with. How is YOUR content going to be better than those already occupying the top 10 in Google? Why should Google rank you above these other pages? What's in it for Google? We talked about this earlier in the book. You need to come up with your own unique angle for the content. Something that Google will want to show its visitors. Something that your visitors will want to share with their friends and followers. What makes your content "share bait"?

Checkpoint #2 - Title

The first thing someone will see when they land on a web page is the page title. In fact, the first thing someone is likely to see BEFORE they get to your site is the title – as that is displayed in the Google search results.

The temptation with the title is to try to include the main phrase you want to rank for, and that can still work well from an SEO point of view. However, remember two things:

1. Your title will be visible in the Google search results, so make sure it is enticing to those who are searching. Will the title arouse curiosity enough to encourage the click through to your page? Think about the last time you read a newspaper or magazine. What was it about certain articles that made you want to read them? There's a good chance it was the title. If your page is shown at the top of the Google SERPs, you are competing with 9 other pages on the exact same topic. How is your title going to encourage searchers to click to your page, rather than a competitor's page? There is no point ranking in the top 10 if no one clicks your link!

2. As we saw earlier, including the exact keyword terms we want to rank for is not important. A lot of the top ranked pages for any particular term do not

include the term in the title, or anywhere else on the page. The THEME is the important thing here, not a specific keyword phrase.

My advice is to go and see what your competitors are using for their titles, and try to come up with a better one. I'd also recommend you choose your title AFTER you have written your content, because it's only then that know the full scope of your content, and how you can sell it using the title.

Let me give you an example.

If I was writing an article on the safety of the Atkins diet, I would search Google for a relevant search phrase, and see what the top 10 are using for titles. These are the titles I have to beat.

Here are the first 5 search results:

atkins diet safety	🎤	🔍

Web   News   Images   Shopping   Videos   More ▾   Search tools

About 546,000 results (0.54 seconds)

Atkins Diet - Does It Work? - US News Best Diets
health.usnews.com/best-**diet**/**atkins**-**diet** ▾ U.S. News & World Report ▾
Jan 3, 2014 - The low-carb **Atkins diet** leaves much to be desired. It's effective ... Easy
to Follow. Nutrition. **Safety**. For Diabetes. For Heart Health. Scores are ...
Atkins Diet Menu - Atkins Diet Recipes - Eco-Atkins Diet - Heart Problems

Atkins Diet Plan Review: Foods, Benefits, and Risks - WebMD
www.webmd.com/**diet**/**atkins**-**diet**-what-it-is ▾ WebMD ▾
Read the **Atkins Diet** review and find out about the foods allowed on this diet plan and
whether it's effective.

Atkins Diet: What's behind the claims? - Mayo Clinic
www.mayoclinic.org/healthy.../in.../**atkins**-**diet**/art-20048485 ▾ Mayo Clinic ▾
May 30, 2014 - **Atkins Diet** — Get the facts about this commercial weight-loss diet. ...
leaders to deliver compassionate, high-value, **safe** patient care. Choose a ...

Is the Atkins diet safe? | Bupa UK
www.bupa.co.uk › ... › Health information › Health features › 2003 ▾ Bupa ▾
May 30, 2003 - The **Atkins diet**, which is based on consuming high levels of protein and
low ... Are there still **safety** issues and is the diet a suitable approach for ...

10 Things Dietitians Say About Low-Carb Diets That Don't ...
authoritynutrition.com › Low-Carb Diet ▾
by Kris Gunnars - Apr 22, 2013 - There are many myths out there about **low-carb diets**,
even among ... I often hear claims that **low-carb diets** are not proven to be **safe** in the
long ...

If I was actually searching for this information, which of those titles stand out?

Only the 4ᵗʰ title is relevant to my search term – "Is the Atkins diet safe?"

I am sure #4 is the one I would click on. However, if I was interested in the safety of
the diet, how much more appealing would be a headline like:

- Atkins diet may be bad for your heart.
- Atkins diet raises bad cholesterol.
- Atkins diet linked with cardiovascular disease.

Now, I have no idea whether the Atkins diet is safe or not, but if I was writing an article on this topic, I would know, and I could structure my headline to make an "emotional" link with the searcher. If it is a safe diet, then headlines like these might make that connection:

- See this evidence. Atkins is safe!
- Heart disease? Not if you follow the Atkins diet properly.
- Why the Atkins Diet is safe.

A few ideas to help with titles/headlines

- Promises to answer a question the searcher has, e.g. "Find out why…."
- Offer benefits, e.g. "Want more free time? …." or "Save $….."
- Avoid pain, or accomplish something, e.g. "Learn how to …… in 3 short steps", "Don't get caught by …", "Avoid….", "Stop pain in its tracks with..", "10 ways to beat.."
- Good headlines are often personal and aimed at the reader. You can do this by talking directly to the reader and using the word "YOU".
- Appeal on the emotional level to the reader (make them feel an emotion as they read your title).
- Make them curious. E.g. "Ever wonder why….", "How do ……?", "How can they get away with…."

OK, so what about title length?

Well, I'd recommend you keep the title as concise as possible. Google tend to show the first 50-60 characters of a title, then replace the rest with ".." (see the final result in the previous screenshot for an example).

To summarize titles, create headlines that arouse interest, keep them concise and not more than 55 - 60 characters in length.

Checkpoint #3 - Filename

If you are using Wordpress, you probably don't give your filenames any thought, since Wordpress will automatically create the filename based on the title of the post.

In Wordpress, a post with the title "See this evidence. Atkins is safe!" would be assigned the filename "see-this-evidence-atkins-is-safe".

Now, there is nothing wrong with that filename. However, I do like to change the filename a little to make it different from the default title conversion. I would probably rename this filename to "evidence-that-atkins-is-safe". This tells Google that a human is more likely to have created the title and filename, rather than a default setting of a script. With Google's obsession for quality content, this small measure might just help with SEO, if not now, then in the future.

In fact, by default, Wordpress will use the post title in:

- The page's "title tag",
- The opening headline of the post,
- The filename.

So, if you don't change the filename (or title tag), you will end up with the same phrases in three place:

Google knows that Wordpress tries to automate things like this, and it is my opinion that automation, even on this small scale, can make your site look less professional. Where you can override this type of automation, I recommend you do, and it is easy enough to change the filename to make it a little different. Some SEOs simply remove the "stop" words from the filename (these are small words like "the", "of", etc).

Therefore the title "evidence-that-atkins-is-safe", would become "evidence-atkins-safe".

Checkpoint #4 – Meta Tags?

In the last checkpoint, we mentioned the "title tag". All web pages should have a "title tag", and Google uses it in the search results as the hyperlinked title to the webpage.

However, there are other tags called Meta tags that you can add to your web pages. Two of the most common ones are the Meta Description and Meta Keywords.

In the source code of a web page, these look like this:

<title>The title of the web page</title>

<meta name="description" content="A description of the the web page">

<meta name="keywords" content="Keywords related to the web page">

The Meta description tag should be a description of the web page content. Google may or may not use this description when they list your page in the SERPs, it all depends on what someone searches for, and whether their search string is found in the description. If it is, then the meta description will probably be used, otherwise a relevant string (containing the search string if it's found) from the main content will be chosen.

I would highly recommend you add the meta description to all important pages on your website. I'd also recommend that you make the Meta description unique. That is, the text of the Meta description is not used anywhere else on the site.

Make sure the Meta description is unique for every single page on your site. Never get lazy and use a generic description on multiple pages.

As you write the Meta description for a page, think of it as a short pre-sell paragraph, telling potential visitors why they should visit the page. If you slip in a bit of niche vocabulary even better, though do write the description for the visitor, not the search engines.

OK, so what about the Meta Keywords tag?

A few years back, this tag was used by Google to help rank pages. If a keyword was in the Meta Keywords tag, the page had a better chance of ranking. Today, the major search engines no longer use the keyword tag to positively affect rankings. However, it is my belief that Google will use the Meta keyword tag to spot "webspam" and penalize it. Anyone that stuffs the Meta Keyword tag with dozens of keywords is a spammer, right? You might not think so, but Google does, so don't do it. My recommendation is to ignore the Meta Keyword tag altogether and not bother with it. If you do want to use it, just include 4 or 5 unique (not synonyms) and relevant keywords.

Checkpoint #5 - Opening Headline

We considered the page title earlier, and saw how important it was to create a concise title that encouraged the click from the search engines.

The opening headline on your page needs the same kind of attention. When someone lands on your page, you want them to read the title and think "Wow, I want to read this."

If you are using Wordpress, then the chances are your opening headline will be the page/post title. That's fine, and if you created a great title, you'll have a great opening headline.

However, if you are building your site in HTML, then you have total control over the page title and opening headline. If you want to make them different, you can. In this case, follow the same rules for creating the opening headline as we did for the page title. Make it short and compelling to encourage your visitors to read your content.

OK, so let's consider a technical aspect of the headline.

The opening headline on each webpage should be an H1 header.

If you are building your site in HTML, then you have total control over which HTML tag is used to display the headline, and of course, the headline itself (giving you the opportunity to make it different from the web page title tag we mentioned earlier).

However, if you are using Wordpress, then your post title will be used for the opening headline, and the Wordpress theme you are using will determine whether that opening headline is an H1 tag, or something else. I have seen a number of Wordpress themes that inexplicably use an H2 for the opening headline. Why?

As with any other written material, the first headline should be the biggest, and that is what an H1 tag is for. The H1 is also given special attention by search engines. Therefore, make sure your Wordpress theme uses the H1 for the opening headline.

It is also important that there is only ONE H1 headline on a page. After the opening H1 headline, use H2 sub-headlines and then H3s if you need a third level to sub-divide an H2 section of content.

You can use multiple H2s and even multiple H3s. However, there must only be ONE H1.

Checkpoint #6 - Theme the content

The words and phrases you use in your content will help Google determine what your content is about, and help them make an initial judgment on quality. Important points to remember include:

1. Does your content contain the niche vocabulary relevant to the topic you are writing about?
2. When you read the content, does it read well for a human, or are there areas where you feel keywords or phrases have been inserted just for the search engines. This is usually easy to spot, because the content doesn't read naturally and seems "forced".
3. Have you use niche vocabulary in the titles and headings of your content? This is something you need to be careful about, since we don't want to keyword stuff the headings. If you can naturally fit in a keyword or phrase into your headline and section headers, do it, but make it natural, and write your

headlines for your visitor, not the search engine. See the previous section on "Opening Heading" above for more tips and help.

As we have said before, if you are an expert in your niche, you don't need to focus on niche vocabulary. You will automatically use it as you write about the subject you know very well.

If you are an expert in the topic you are writing about, you can skip directly to the part of checkpoint #6 called "Checking your Theme".

But what if you are not an expert?

Well, in that case, you already have the niche vocabulary that you collected for your content. Check back on the chapter about niche vocabulary if you haven't completed that step yet.

Let's look at an example, based on the niche vocabulary I collected earlier in the book, so we can see how to use it naturally as we write.

We looked that the case of diabetes, and how the niche vocabulary changed slightly as we looked at each type in turn. Here are the words and phrases related to gestational diabetes:

Diabetes, insulin, glucose, blood, type, levels, sugar, diet, insulin resistance, non-insulin dependent, adult-onset, obesity, gestational, pregnancy, baby, risk to baby, risks to mother, women, pregnant

The first thing I recommend you do with your list is to make sure you understand all of the words and phrases. It's impossible to write a good piece of content if we don't understand the words we are using. It also helps to understand the vocabulary as you start planning out your piece of content. Go and find out how each phrase relates to gestational diabetes?

With a better understanding of the words and phrases, my next step is to check out the top 10 results ranking for the topic, and see what they cover. Making a note of the headlines used in these pages can help guide you in the structure of your own content. However, remember you are always on the lookout for an idea that will make your content stand out.

Here are the headlines from the top 10 pages in Google ranking for gestational diabetes. You will see some headline repeated because they are used on more than one page:

Gestational Diabetes - Caring for yourself and your baby

Causes

Symptoms

Exams and tests

Treatment

Outlook

When to contact a medical professional

Prevention

Alternative names

What is gestational diabetes?

Who gets gestational diabetes, and why do I have to be tested

What should I expect during my test?

If I have gestational diabetes how will I be treated?

Is there anything I should be afraid of?

Recommended reading

Diabetes of pregnancy

Why insulin is important

What can gestational diabetes do to me and my child?

Am I at risk of developing gestational diabetes?

What can be done about gestational diabetes?

As you can see, a number of headlines are repeated or very similar.

If Google is ranking these pages in the top 10, then the subject matter of these top 10 pages is what Google thinks is most relevant for the search term. Therefore these headings give us a great starting point for structuring our own content, because they tell us what we need to cover.

If we try to condense this list down by grouping similar headlines, we end up with something like this:

What is Gestational Diabetes?

What can gestational diabetes do to me and my child?

Who Is at Risk for Gestational Diabetes?

What Causes Gestational Diabetes in Pregnancy?

Why insulin is important

How common is gestational diabetes?

Symptoms

What Are the Complications of Gestational Diabetes?

When to see a doctor

Screening - non-challenge blood glucose tests, oral glucose tolerance test, urinary glucose testing, What should I expect during my test?

Treatment & Outlook

Recommended reading

I've put the headlines in an order that makes sense to me. What I have listed above is a skeleton structure for my own article, listing all of the important points I need to cover. If there is just too much to cover in a single article, then I could split it into two or more articles and link them together as part 1, part 2, etc. However, I like longer content and I wouldn't split anything below around 2500 words.

As I was going through the headlines of the top 10, one article stood out to me, because the headlines were a little different. Here they are:

What Is Gestational Diabetes?

Who Gets Gestational Diabetes, And Why Do I Have To Be Tested?

What Should I Expect During My Test?

If I Have Gestational Diabetes How Will I Be Treated?

Is There Anything I Should Be Afraid Of?

These headlines are talking directly to the expectant mother and use the word "I". I believe these headlines would connect on an emotional level with the visitor, who presumably wants to know how gestational diabetes would affect them, or their family or friend who is pregnant. All of the other 9 pages in the top 10 used impersonal and "scientific" headlines, what we called earlier a journalistic or fact based writing style. If you were a pregnant mum looking for answers, wouldn't you like the article to speak to you as an expectant mother, rather than just get a list of facts?

This more personal approach to headlines is nice, and in this example, I think it's the first step in making the content more unique, and stand out.

OK, with the article mapped out, the next step is writing it.

This is where theme words and phrases become important, but the most important thing to remember is that you need to write naturally, for your audience. Don't obsess over keywords and phrases, as they will be used naturally, IF you understand what the words mean and how they are associated with the topic.

To start, I would come up with a working title. I might change it once the article is finished, but a working headline can keep you focused and on task.

My working headline might be something like:

Gestational Diabetes – Your questions answered

This title implies that the article talks directly to the pregnant woman, and answers her questions. It also gets the main phrase "gestational diabetes" in at the start – they are the first words Google see!

Other headlines that would work include:

"Everything you need to know about gestational diabetes"

"Gestational diabetes – are you at risk and how will it affect you?"

"Am I at risk of gestational diabetes?"

"How will gestational diabetes affect me?"

All of these headlines contain references to "you" or "I", implying they are more personal and directed at real people.

My next step would be to work my way through each headline, writing a paragraph of content for each one. I would try to use the word "I" in each of the section headlines wherever possible, to mimic the actual questions pregnant women have during their pregnancy.

So instead of this:

"Who Is at Risk for Gestational Diabetes?"

I would use

"Am I at risk of gestational diabetes?"

Instead of:

"Screening"

I'd use:

"How will I be tested?"

As you write each paragraph of your article, concentrate on covering the material in a natural way. Do not try to add keywords simply because you know you need to theme your content. As you work on your content, you will find that the theme words work their way in naturally.

Working with Theme Phrases

You may have found a list of 10-15 theme phrases during your research. DO NOT try to insert them all into your article. Typically, I'll only use 3-5 theme phrases in a long article, and those are the more important phrases. Far more important than the theme phrases, are the words that make up those phrases.

For example we identified the phrases "risk to baby" and "risks to mother". There is absolutely no need to use both of those phrases in your article. In fact, you don't need to use either of them. You will be talking about the mother, you will be talking about the baby, and you will also be talking about "risks". You might say something like:

"There are some risks associated with gestational diabetes that can affect you, the mother, and your baby."

That is fine from a theme point of view as you talk about the risks to the mother and the baby, even though you don't use the exact phrases. The fact that the words "risk", "baby" and "mother" are in the same sentence, means the words that make up the phrases are close together (proximity). The search engines look at word proximity to help determine meaning. Therefore if there are any important word combinations (e.g. baby and risk(s)), putting them in close proximity can give the search engines a helping hand without having to try to stuff theme phrases into your content.

Someone writing specifically for the search engines might write something like this:

"Gestational diabetes can be dangerous when you are pregnant and has risks to mother and a risk to baby."

This is grammatically incorrect and just doesn't flow very well. It's obvious the writer was trying to get the two exact phrases into the sentence, yet it really isn't necessary.

At all times, write for the visitor, not for the search engine.

When you finish your article, you should check the theme.

Checking your Theme

The first thing you should do is read through your article and make sure it flows well. Will a human enjoy reading it? Are there any awkward parts that need to be re-worked? Have you used any phrases that don't fit naturally, and would be better off split into the component words and re-written as a different sentence (like the risks/baby/mother example above).

OK, now go through your niche vocabulary. Have you used all of the keywords in your article? You certainly do not have to use all of them, but make sure you have used the most important ones. For phrases, don't worry if you've only used one or two. As we mentioned above, the words that make up the phrases are generally more important, and if there is a really important phrase, get it in there, or at least write a sentence that uses all of the words in that phrase, so the words are in close proximity.

A good final check for theme is to head on over to the Google Keyword Planner.

Click on **Search for new keyword and ad group ideas.**

Paste the URL of your article into the **Your landing page** box:

What would you like to do?

▾ Search for new keyword and ad group ideas

Enter one or more of the following:

Your product or service

> For example, flowers or used cars

Your landing page

> http://americanpregnancy.org/pregnancycomplications/gestationaldiabetes.html

Your product category

> Enter or select a product category ▾

Targeting ?

All locations	✎
English	✎
Google	✎
Negative keywords	✎

Date range ?

> Show avg. monthly searches for: Last 12 months ✎

Customize your search ?

Keyword filters ✎

Keyword options ✎
Show broadly related ideas
Hide keywords in my account
Hide keywords in my plan

Include/Exclude ✎

Get ideas

Click the **Get Ideas** button at the bottom, and see what "Ad Group Ideas" and "Keyword Ideas" are returned. Here are some of the ad groups returned for a good article on gestational diabetes:

```
Baby Diabetes
Blood Glucose
Blood Levels
Blood Sugar
Control Blood
Control Pregnancy
Diabetes
Diabetes After
Diabetes Association
Diabetes Complications
Diabetes Diet
Diabetes During
Diabetes In Pregnancy
Diabetes Normal
Diabetes Symptoms
Diabetes Testing
Diabetes Treatment
Diabetes Type
Glucose Levels
Glucose Test
Good Blood
Have Gestational
Keywords like: American Diet Association
Levels Diabetes
Levels Gestational
Levels Pregnant
Monitoring Blood
Normal Glucose
Normal Sugar
Pregnancy
Pregnancy Diet
Pregnancy Doctor
Pregnancy Gestational
Pregnancy Glucose
```

And on the keyword ideas tab:

Keyword (by relevance)	Avg. monthly searches [?]	Competition [?]
diabetes during pregnancy	2,900	Low
diabetes in pregnancy	5,400	Low
diabetic and pregnant	210	Low
diabetes when pregnant	480	Low
diabetes and pregnancy	2,900	Low

Clearly Google thinks this article is about diabetes during pregnancy.

You can test your content at Google Keyword Planner to see if Google correctly recognizes your theme. If there are any ad groups or phrases that seem wrong, go back to your article and see if you can see why Google is getting confused about your theme.

Checkpoint #7 - Above the Fold

Remember when we talked about the important Google algorithm changes? One update that occurred in January 2012 is very important to remember - the page layout algorithm, often called the "top heavy" update.

It is important to think how your web page will look like as soon as someone lands on it, and before they scroll down the page. This area of your web page is called the "above the fold" region.

The "above the fold" region is dependent on the screen resolution of the visitor. If a visitor is coming to your site with a screen resolution of 640 x 480, they might only see this:

Whereas a visitor with a screen resolution of 1024 x 768 would see this:

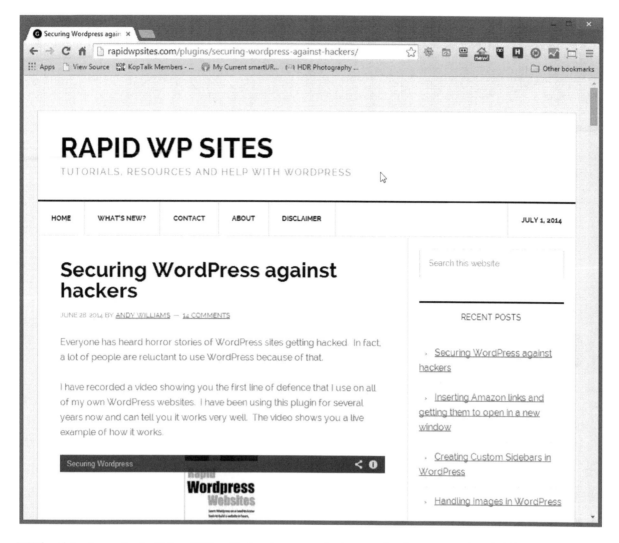

With this in mind, it's difficult to know what resolution you should be testing your own pages with. However, by looking at this page:

http://www.w3schools.com/browsers/browsers_display.asp

Only 1% of people use a screen resolution of 800x 600 or lower, so if you assume a resolution of 1024 x 768 and test your pages with that, you know you'll be covering 99% of your visitors.

OK, so what is the deal with the "above the fold" area?

Google want this area to contain "content", and by content, I mean the stuff the visitor has come to find. What they don't want is the above the fold to be mainly advertising, like this site:

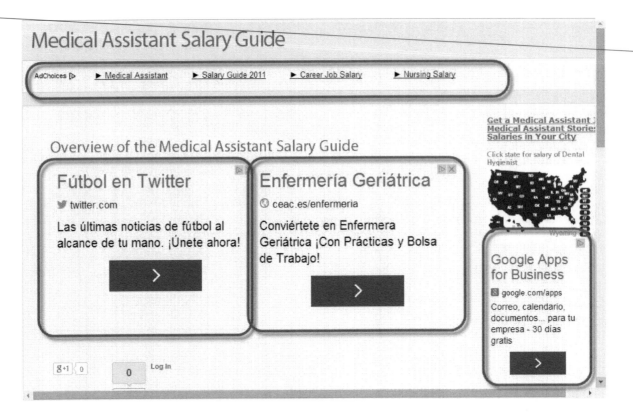

I've drawn boxes around all of the adverts. Where is the content? Actually there isn't any on that page, but on another page of the same site you can sees some "content" if you scroll far enough.

Medical Assistant Salary Guide

From Job Hopping to a Stable Career in Medical Assisting

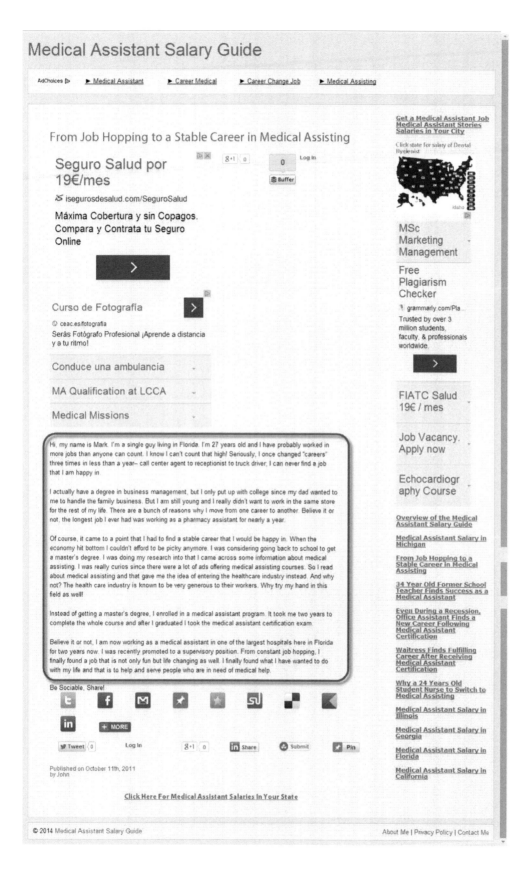

Hi, my name is Mark. I'm a single guy living in Florida. I'm 27 years old and I have probably worked in more jobs than anyone can count. I know I can't count that high! Seriously, I once changed "careers" three times in less than a year-- call center agent to receptionist to truck driver; I can never find a job that I am happy in.

I actually have a degree in business management, but I only put up with college since my dad wanted to me to handle the family business. But I am still young and I really didn't want to work in the same store for the rest of my life. There are a bunch of reasons why I move from one career to another. Believe it or not, the longest job I ever had was working as a pharmacy assistant for nearly a year.

Of course, it came to a point that I had to find a stable career that I would be happy in. When the economy hit bottom I couldn't afford to be picky anymore. I was considering going back to school to get a master's degree. I was doing my research into that I came across some information about medical assisting. I was really curios since there were a lot of ads offering medical assisting courses. So I read about medical assisting and that gave me the idea of entering the healthcare industry instead. And why not? The health care industry is known to be very generous to their workers. Why try my hand in this field as well!

Instead of getting a master's degree, I enrolled in a medical assistant program. It took me two years to complete the whole course and after I graduated I took the medical assistant certification exam.

Believe it or not, I am now working as a medical assistant in one of the largest hospitals here in Florida for two years now. I was recently promoted to a supervisory position. From constant job hopping, I finally found a job that is not only fun but life changing as well. I finally found what I have wanted to do with my life and that is to help and serve people who are in need of medical help.

Click Here For Medical Assistant Salaries in Your State

115

Anyone landing on the page would only see adverts. This particular site was designed that way, its only purpose to get people clicking adverts. Before the Page Layout algorithm was introduced, this page probably did OK with Adsense income, but since January 2012, I doubt it gets any traffic other than from people curious to see how NOT to do it.

At the other end of the spectrum is this page:

Where is the content?

This page is as bad as the previous one. There is nothing above the fold, and I doubt this was done by design. However, it will also suffer the consequences of Google's page layout algorithm.

What is above the fold on your pages?

Make sure it is valuable content. You can have an advert above the fold, but make sure your content is what really shines in that region.

While we are talking about the top of your webpage, it is also worth considering something else.

The top of your article needs to do a lot of hard work to convince the visitor that the page is worth reading. The headline needs to grab their attention, and the opening paragraph needs to pique their interest. If you fail to make that first impression, the visitor may well just hit the back button to Google, and that "bounce" will tell Google that your page did not satisfy them. You can guess what would happen next...

Checkpoint #8 - Help the skimmers

A lot of people visiting your site will be "skimmers". In other words, they don't want to read the whole page to find out if it is something they are interested in. They want to skim the page. If they see something that catches their attention, then they'll read it, otherwise they'll head on back to Google.

It is therefore always a good idea to help the skimmers by breaking up large blocks of text with "skimmables".

Definition ☺: Skimmables - stuff that help the skimmer ascertain their interest levels.

The best way to do this is to break up your text with:

- Sub-headings (H2, H3),
- Images where they can complement the text (or even replace a paragraph),
- Bullet points. Bullet points are a skimmer's dream, since they are used to highlight points in an easily skimmable format.

As you write your content, always remember the skimmers.

Checkpoint #9 - Grammar & Spelling

In the old days of SEO, webmasters would intentionally spell words incorrectly in the hope of ranking for misspelled search queries at Google. Those days are long gone, and it is now important to make sure your content is grammatically correct with good spelling.

Bad grammar can be an indicator of poor quality content, and Google do look at spelling and grammar. While it is unlikely they would directly penalize content with minor mistakes, they would probably take notice of visitor feedback and could penalize pages or sites their users complain about.

Google would almost certainly penalize a page or site, if they thought it deliberately used incorrect spelling or grammar in an attempt to increase search rankings.

Checkpoint #10 - Check the quality

The final checkpoint I want you to think about is a simple quality check on all content you publish on your website.

One of the best ways to do this is to read your content aloud, either to yourself, or better still to a friend.

How does it flow? Are there any sentences or paragraphs you need to re-read to make sense of them, or the odd word that trips you up?

As you read through the content, are there any words or phrases (especially those that you want to rank for in Google) that seem to be repeated too many times (keyword stuffing)? When you read a phrase and remember having just said that exact same phrase moments earlier, you know it's being used too often.

Or, perhaps the phrase doesn't flow well within the sentence and would be better changed for a synonym. Perhaps you are aware that you only used a specific phrase because you were thinking about the search engines, and what you wanted to rank for?

Imagine giving the article to another webmaster, and asking them "Can you tell what words and phrases I want to rank for in Google?" If they can, then chances are you need to re-work your content.

Always write for your visitor, not for Google.

Another thing you should think about as you check your article for quality is whether or not visitors will trust the content. I always find that visitors trust web pages more when they know who wrote them. Is there a face behind the web page? An author resource box with photo is a great idea as it really helps build confidence in your visitors.

Another quality issue is "fluff". This is a common element of poor content. Essentially, it's sentences or paragraphs that really don't say anything new. Maybe they repeat a point that was made earlier, or they only seem to be there to increase word count. Nobody likes reading fluff, so strip it out of your content.

Look carefully at the "hidden" elements of the web page. Hopefully you won't have done any of the following. In fact, if you don't understand what I mean in these bullet points, so much the better.

Check:

- ALT tags on images. Make sure these accurately describe the image to help vision impaired visitors. DO NOT stuff them with keywords.
- Does your HTML use comment tags? If so, are these necessary, e.g. to explain to someone else working on the site why you made changes? Or are they stuffed with keyword-rich text that will get you into trouble with Google?
- Is there any text on your page that is "hidden"? Or maybe you've got hidden links (e.g. hyperlinked a full stop/period on the page to try to pass some link juice to another page)?
- If you have hyperlinks on the page, have you stuffed the title attribute with keywords?
  e.g. <a href=http://somedomain.com title="keywords typically stuffed here">My Link</a>

  I'd recommend you don't use the title attribute when creating hyperlinks, as the title attribute has been heavily abused in the past by web spammers. If you do want to use it, use it as it was meant to be used - to explain the nature of the link so visitors see a descriptive "tool tip" when they hover their mouse over it.

As a general summarizing rule for this checkpoint:

Remove anything on your web page, visible or otherwise, that is only there for the benefit of the search engines.

Additional Considerations

The main checkpoints will keep you on the road to quality content, but I have a few other suggestions that you might like to incorporate.

Link to authority sites?

If you mention something in your content that you learned on another site, give that site a mention with a link (you can nofollow the link if you want to, but I tend not to if that site is a true authority on the topic) just like research papers cite other papers. The internet is meant to be a "web" of content and Google like this type of natural link. It is exactly the type of link you hope others will give your content.

Further reading

At the end of any piece of content, you can offer your visitors a "further reading" section. This can contain links to interesting articles, videos, infographics, etc, either on your site or on other authority sites (open external links in new windows).

A photo of the author & bio box?

Visitors love to know who wrote the content, so a photo and short author bio is a really good idea. It builds trust, and trust is vital in the online environment. If you are using Wordpress to build your site, there are themes that have author boxes built in, and plugins for those themes that don't.

Links to related content on your site

If someone reads to the end of a piece of content on your site, they probably liked it. Therefore, at the end of the content, offer them a list of related article on your site, that you think they might also be interested in. A list of 3 or 4 "related posts" is always a good idea.

Here is an example. I wrote an article on one of my sites called "Createspace - Basic Text Formatting". This article was written for people who want to publish a book on Amazon's Createspace platform. At the end of the article, I had this related posts section:

Related Posts:

1. 2. WYSIWYG – Createspace Word document to PDF
2. 5. The TOC
3. 6. Adding a new title to Createspace

These three links are all related to publishing on Createspace, so anyone that read my "Basic Text Formatting" would probably also be interested in these articles.

For Wordpress users there are a number of plugins that can automatically create these "Related Post" sections on your pages. For non-Wordpress users, you can create these sections manually in HTML code.

Related posts sections like this, help to keep visitors on your site longer, and this is something Google take note of.

Allow comments

Visitors like to interact and leave feedback or ask questions. For that reason, I recommend you allow visitors to leave comments. Again, Wordpress users will find this easy to implement because comments are built into the Wordpress platform.

For non-Wordpress users, there are scripts you can use to create a comment section on your web pages. I cannot recommend any, because I use Wordpress for my own websites, but searching Google for "comments script" should turn up some options.

Allow social sharing & following

We are trying to create "Share Bait", so give your visitors an easy way to share your content. The next chapter shows how.

Social Sharing Buttons

If you think in terms of creating "share bait" (people like it so much that they want to share it), you need to offer your visitors an easy way to share your content. The main social networks offer buttons that you can put on your website, and if you use Wordpress, there are a number of plugins that can automate the set up of social sharing buttons.

As a starting point, I recommend you have buttons to share your content on Google+, Twitter and Facebook. StumbleUpon is also important as it can send good content viral. If you have a lot of images on your site that you want shared, then Pinterest is a good button to include. However, if the images on your site are not a main focus point, I'd leave Pinterest out.

Adding Social Share buttons to a non-Wordpress site

If you want an easy option, you can use a service like http://www.addtoany.com/ or http://www.sharethis.com/ which will give you the code to put onto your website. You can customize the buttons in the code that these services give you, though be aware that most services will add a button or link back to their own website. If that is not acceptable to you, you'll need to visit the individual networks, and grab the HTML code for each network in turn to add to your site.

Where to get social sharing buttons:

Editing HTML is beyond the scope of this book, but I assume, if you run an HTML website you are happy editing HTML. Therefore I have listed the URLs below where you can get the main social sharing buttons for your site. Follow the instructions on these pages to add the code to your site.

Twitter
Twitter: https://about.twitter.com/resources/buttons

Facebook
Facebook follow: https://developers.facebook.com/docs/plugins/follow-button

Facebook like button: https://developers.facebook.com/docs/plugins/like-button

Facebook like box: https://developers.facebook.com/docs/plugins/like-box-for-pages

Google Plus
Google Plus follow: https://developers.google.com/+/web/follow/

Google Plus Plus One button: https://developers.google.com/+/web/+1button/

Google Plus Share: https://developers.google.com/+/web/share/

StumbleUpon
Stumble Upon share: http://www.stumbleupon.com/dt/badges/create

Pinterest
Pinterest follow:

http://business.pinterest.com/en/widget-builder#do_follow_me_button

Pinterest Pin It:

http://business.pinterest.com/en/widget-builder#do_pin_it_button

Adding Social Share buttons to a Wordpress website

If you use Wordpress, then adding the social sharing buttons to your site is as easy as installing and activating a plugin. After that, set up is usually a case of selecting which buttons you want to display and you're done.

There are so many plugins to choose from, but I have listed a couple of the ones that I use, where to get them, and why I like them. If you have your own personal favourite, go with that instead.

Once a social sharing plugin is installed, visit the plugin settings page to set up the plugin, selecting only those social networks you want to offer your visitors.

WP Socialite
You can find this plugin here:

http://wordpress.org/plugins/wpsocialite/

Why I like this plugin:

1. Simple to use.
2. Fast loading – in fact it can be set to load only when a user scrolls to the area the buttons are displayed, meaning faster loading times for your main site content.

Fast & Easy Social Sharing
You can find this plugin here:

http://wordpress.org/plugins/fast-easy-social-sharing/

Why I like this plugin:

1. Simple to use.
2. Loads the icons as fonts, so is extremely fast. No JavaScript is loaded from any of the social networks, and that speeds up the loading of the buttons as only the font and stylesheet need to be called to show the buttons.
3. I love the look of the buttons:

If you want to watch a short tutorial on installing and configuring these plugins, I created one here:

http://rapidwpsites.com/tutorials/adding-social-sharing-buttons-to-your-website

Adding "Fat" to your site

The term "fat" in the title of this section is used deliberately because of Google's own use of the word "thin", essentially meaning a site with very little substance and poor content.

Great content is certainly a good start, but there are other "features" you can add to a site that will:

- Encourage a visitor to share your content
- Encourage a visitor to recommend your site
- Encourage a visitor to return
- Encourage a visitor to interact with you, and/or other visitors
- Start increasing your authority in the visitor's eyes
- Tell Google that you are worth listening to

I want to go through a few ideas for you to think about. These are in no particular order.

An autoresponder and/or newsletter

When you first meet someone, you don't always trust them, do you? As you meet that person again and again, trust has a chance to grow, but it will usually take several meetings. The same trust issues exist online.

Why would someone visiting your website trust you enough to buy something on your site, or something that you recommend? Of course, as you create wonderful fat websites, trust will grow, but that can take quite some time. Autoresponders allow us to speed up the trust process.

An autoresponder is a series of pre-written emails that you can send out to people who sign up for them.

These emails can be scheduled to be sent at any interval you like. So you could send one a day, one a week or once a month. You could also send one a day for a week, then one a week for the next few months, and finally go to a once a month schedule.

The emails in an autoresponder can be anything you like, but the best way to use them initially is to build trust. If it takes 6 or 7 meetings to trust someone, then think of the first 6 or 7 emails as a trust building exercise. Offer great value, and don't ask for much, if anything, in return.

Here are a few examples of how I have use autoresponders:

- To sell a piece of software. Software is created to make our lives easier, right? First off, I'd identify the various tasks that the software carried out, helping users save time. I'd then setup 5 – 6 emails, each with a tutorial on how to carry out these specific tasks the long way. I wouldn't even mention the software at that stage. After 5 or 6 emails, trust is starting to build, so I could then introduce the software and show how it can do those tasks easier and faster than manually.
- To sell a course. Similar to the first example, but the emails would contain tutorials that "whet the appetite". I would send out 5 or 6 tutorials before introducing the benefits of the course.
- To offer free courses to my visitors. I'd recommend tools in the course and use affiliate links to promote them. For example, I might have a course on creating video tutorials with Camtasia Studio, and link to Camtasia Studio with an affiliate link. Since anyone on the course needs the software, they might buy through my link, earning me a commission.

I am sure you can think of lots of examples in your own niche, but if you struggle to come up with ideas, visit your competitor sites, and see if any of those have sign up forms. Some may be for a newsletter, some may be for an autoresponder. If I find an autoresponder on a popular website, I'll sign up for it, see what they are doing and come out with my own twist on their idea.

The autoresponder service I use is called Aweber.

http://ezseonews.aweber.com/

One of the benefits of this type of service is that not only can you set up autoresponders, but you can also offer a newsletter. A newsletter is similar, meaning you can send an email to anyone that has signed up to receive it. However, I usually differentiate between newsletters and autoresponders as follows:

- An autoresponder is pre-written and scheduled for delivery in the future.
- A newsletter is written at the moment you want to send it, and usually sent immediately, or scheduled for later in the day.

Not everyone would agree with my differentiation here, but it works well for me because it gives me an opportunity to explain how I use both – differently.

Let's take the example of a cooking website. The webmaster might set up an autoresponder with 52 free recipes. If he scheduled them to be delivered at the rate of one per week, then when someone signs up for the free recipes, they'll start receiving one per week for a year. That's right. As long as that person remains subscribed to the autoresponder, the webmaster has their attention, on a weekly basis, for a whole year!

Now, let's suppose the webmaster is running a sale on cooking pots. He could write a newsletter two days before his promotion was due to run, letting his recipe subscribers know about the forthcoming sale. When the sale started, he could send another newsletter telling his list that the sale was on.

Those that signed up for the recipes should be quite targeted, since they signed up for recipes. That means the webmaster has a targeted audience he can tap into any time he wants. When the year of recipes run out for a subscriber, they stay on the list and will continue to get newsletters until they unsubscribe.

Hopefully you can see the power in an autoresponder. To my mind, they are one of the most important features for any website.

A Forum

We all know what a forum is, but did you ever think of adding one to your own website? Growing a community of like-minded people, offering them a place to meet up and chat about anything, is a great way to build visitor loyalty to your site.

OK, so you think it's too difficult to set up, right? Well, if you don't have a Wordpress website, it is a little complicated, though most forum software companies will help you through it.

Popular forum scripts include:

- http://www.vbulletin.com/
- http://www.invisionpower.com/
- https://www.phpbb.com/

If your site is powered by Wordpress, there is a "free" plugin that can add a forum to your site. I have added a few more details of this plugin to the "Wordpress Plugins" chapter later in the book.

Infographics

We have already talked about the importance of images as a type of content on your site. Infographics are a unique type of image. As the name implies, they are images that convey information, and sometimes it's a lot of information.

Oxford dictionaries define an infographic as:

"A visual representation of information or data, e.g. as a chart or diagram: a good infographic is worth a thousand words."

So why are infographics a good idea?

1. They help you visitor understand your "data" in a visual and often entertaining way.
2. Good infographics often get shared, so it's a good opportunity to get new visitors to your site.
3. You can use the infographic as link bait, offering other webmasters some code that will embed the infographic into their own website, with a link back to yours.

If you want to see examples of infographics, search Google images for "infographics", and you'll a lot of great examples.

There are a number of sites that allow you to create infographics. Three of the most popular ones are:

- http://infogr.am/
- http://create.visual.ly/
- http://piktochart.com/

A lot of these services offer you the chance to start for free, with paid options for those that need more features.

RSS feeds

If you can (and everyone who uses Wordpress can, because it's built in), I would recommend offering your visitors an RSS feed of the important content on your website. Make it obvious to your visitor that you have an RSS feed by showing them the standard RSS "button":

So what is an RSS feed and why bother? Well, we looked briefly at them earlier as a way of monitoring competitor websites in our niche, but let's look in a little more detail.

Essentially an RSS feed is a vehicle for delivering content in a standard format.

That definition may just have confused you, so let me give you an example.

All Wordpress websites have RSS feeds built into them, so let's use a Wordpress site for this example. Any time you create a new post and publish it to your site, the RSS feed (which essentially lists the post's title, URL, date/time published and a short description) is updated to add the new post at the top of the feed. All of the other posts in the feed drop down one place. If your feed is set up to hold 10 items, then adding a new post would cause the 10th item to scroll off the bottom of the feed and be removed as the new post gets top spot. Therefore the feed is always showing your most recent 10 posts.

So why bother with RSS?

Think of RSS feeds as a doorway to your site.

A lot more people stay up to date with their favourite sites using RSS feed readers. The feed reader we saw earlier, and the one I use, is http://feedly.com/ and you can sign up and use it for free. There are also feed readers available for iOS and Android mobile devices.

Savvy visitors to your site may use RSS feeds to keep up to date with their interests. By offering them your RSS feed, any time you post a new piece of content on your site, they get notified of the new content in their feed reader (which has spotted that new post in your feed).

RSS feeds ensure that your new content is pushed to users that follow your feed. That in turn helps build trust if they are getting new content from you on a regular basis.

A lot of people think that RSS feeds are a dying technology, especially in view of the fact that Google closed down its own "Google Reader" tool. It's argued that people don't follow feeds as much as they used to because of Twitter, Facebook and other social channels where good content is shared. However, the fact that it is built into Wordpress means you don't have to set anything up if you use Wordpress. It is already built in, so use it. Offer that feed button on your site.

Quizes, Polls and surveys

People love to get involved, IF it is easy. They'll vote in a poll if it just means clicking a button. Surveys and quizzes can be equally fun, but maybe more difficult to get participants. However, these will add "fat" to your site, and the search engines will like the visitor interaction on your site, so don't dismiss it.

I good poll script to use on non-Wordpress sites is "Advanced Poll", and it's easy to set up, and free.

Advanced Poll: http://www.proxy2.de/scripts.php

You can find a lot of scripts to carry out polls, quizzes and surveys at:

http://www.scripts.com

Look for those with the best ratings, and try them.

For Wordpress users, "Yop Poll" is a popular choice:

https://wordpress.org/plugins/yop-poll/

Software, scripts, calculators, etc

You may not be a programmer, but that does not mean you cannot have software written for you. There are a number of outsourcing websites, like http://odesk.com, which allow you to hire workers for just about anything. I personally do some programming, but that hasn't stopped me outsourcing programming jobs if I was low on time.

So what type of program or script could be of use to your visitors?

Let me give you a few examples.

If you had a site on loans, you could offer your visitors a loan calculator that could tell them how much their repayments would be. Maybe you could offer them a mortgage calculator.

If you had a diet site, you could get a search script created that could tell your visitors how many calories a particular food item has.

Both of these examples offer value to your visitors, and depending on how you designed the scripts, you could give them something that wasn't available on your competitor sites.

Other types of software include downloadable programs that can run on Windows, Mac, Mobile or other operating systems. This is probably something that is more realistic for software companies because of the cost to get complicated software created. However, have a think about any small utility you could get created and open a project on ODesk asking for bids. You might be surprised by the quotes.

An example of a small utility might be a "times tables" generator tool for a math-related site. People could download the tool and generate times table tests for their kids. It's a fairly simply tool that would take an experienced programmer a few hours to create, so wouldn't be that expensive.

If you have software utilities that can be downloaded by your visitors, you can also submit your utilities to software websites, which in return will increase downloads and give you a link back to your website.

Of course, you may want to sell your software utility, and that is fine. You could get a trial version created which would allow your visitors to try before they buy.

Do also consider mobile apps that you can advertise on your site. While these can be expensive to get programmers to create for you, there are a growing number of sites that allow non-programmers to easily build mobile apps, like these ones:

http://www.como.com/

http://appsmoment.com/

http://www.appnotch.com/

You can usually start building your app for free!

Quotations & Trivia

Are there any famous quotations in your niche? Or maybe you have some strange trivia related to your content?

People love trivia. People love famous quotations. Why not include them in your content?

You'd be surprised what you can find online if you look.

You could use quotations or trivia at the start, middle, or end of an article.

To find great trivia, search Google for "dog trivia", or whatever topic you are writing about.

If you can find a lot of trivia on a topic, you could include a "trivia" section at the end of your article. That would certainly catch the eye of even the quickest skimmers.

For example, **Did you know:**

"French Poodles did not originate in France."

"65% of pet owners have more photos of their pet than their spouse."

"70% of pet owners sign their pets name on greeting cards."

"33% of dog owners admit to talking to their dog on the phone or leaving answer machine messages."

Would you like some more dog trivia?

Yes?

Then you get my point about using trivia on your web pages.

A great place to find relevant quotations is http://www.brainyquote.com/

Just type in a word or phrase related to the piece of content you are writing and see if there is anything interesting, amusing or controversial.

Video

Even if you have not recorded and produced your own video for a piece of content you are working on, there are several good video sharing sites that allow you to embed videos created by other people. The best known is obviously Google-owned Youtube.

If you can find fun or informative videos that are closely relevant to your own content, then you can embed those videos into your web page.

On Youtube, look for the **Share** link under the video, and you'll get an "embed code" which needs to be inserted into your web page.

The Making of a Stained Glass Tiffany Lamp

John Berry · 49 videos

46,570

✓ Subscribed ⚙   Share with Hootlet

👍 85   👎 8

👍 Like   👎

About   **Share**   Add to

Share this video   **Embed**   Email

```
<iframe width="480" height="360"
src="//www.youtube.com/embed/SrEIHEp1g5E" frameborder="0"
allowfullscreen></iframe>
```

Video size: 480 × 360   ▼

☑ Show suggested videos when the video finishes

☐ Enable privacy-enhanced mode [?]

☐ Use old embed code [?]

You'll notice that under the embed code, you can select a video size. Check to see how wide the main content column is on your website, and choose a video size that best matches that width.

TIP: Before embedding a video into your own website, watch the video all the way through. That sounds obvious, but you'd be surprised how many people will skip that step and just watch the first minute or two. Make sure that the video is good quality, and isn't packed with advertising to the creators own website. Any video you embed will be a reflection on you and your own site, so only use the best.

I hope this section has given you a few more ideas for making your content "stickier" and more entertaining for your visitors.

Wordpress Plugins that can help improve your site

There are a lot of great plugins that can really help take your site to the next level. In this section, I'll mention a few of the ones I think you should be looking at. I should add that a couple of these plugins are not free.

OnePress Social Locker

This is one of my favourite plugins as it encourages (some might say bribes) your visitors to share your content. This plugin has a free version, but to get the premium features, you need to pay $22 (at the time of writing).

You can see my review of this plugin here:

http://ezseonews.com/review/social-locker-review/

SimplePress Forum

SimplePress is a Wordpress plugin that can add a forum to your website. The basic Simplepress plugin is free, but to get support, plus more advanced features (as add-on plugins), you need to "subscribe". That currently costs $39 for two months membership. As a member, you can download all of the add-on plugins that are available, which extend the features of the SimplePress plugin, giving you a fully featured forum. And don't worry that this is a "membership". You only need to get the 2 month membership ONCE, and you'll receive updates to SimplePress and all of the plugins you've downloaded, even after your membership expires. The only thing you lose when your membership expires is access to support.

Wishlist Member

This is a plugin that can turn your Wordpress site (or a section of it) into a membership site. You can have different levels of members, maybe some free, some paid, with different levels of access. It is a very complete plugin that can integrate with a large number of payment processors.

You can get more details of Wishlist member at:

http://rapidwpsites.com/tutorials/wishlist-member-review/

Formidable Pro

This plugin allows you to create forms for your site.

There is a free basic version and paid versions (starting at $47). The free version is all you need to create a basic contact form, but the paid versions offers you a lot more in terms of customizing forms.

If you want to allow visitors to submit their stories, recipes or any other kind of content, then this is a great plugin. I also use this plugin to create forms that my outsourcers use to submit the content I am hiring them to write, directly to my site. Their submissions become draft posts, that I just need to approve. It saves a lot of time.

You can see a tutorial I recorded on this plugin here:

http://rapidwpsites.com/plugins/formidable-procustom-web-forms/

Hopefully you will have found these plugins interesting and see the potential for adding more value to your website. However, we have just touched the surface of useful plugins out there. You can find a lot more Wordpress plugins here:

https://wordpress.org/plugins/

I also run a website offering free Wordpress tips, tutorials and advice over at:

http://rapidwpsites.com/

Feel free to pop on over and say hello. If you have any questions, I have a contact form and you can even leave suggestions for tutorials you would like to see.

Did you enjoy this book?

If you liked this book (or even if you didn't), PLEASE add a review on the Amazon website. You can find the book listing by searching Amazon for Creating Fat Content.

All the best

Andy Williams

More Information from Dr. Andy Williams

If you would like more information, tips, tutorials or advice, there are two resources you might like to consider.

The first is my free weekly newsletter over at ezSEONews.com offering tips, tutorials and advice to online marketers and webmasters. Just sign up and my newsletter, plus SEO articles, will be delivered to your inbox. I cannot always promise a weekly schedule, but I try ;)

I also run RapidWPSites.com, a website all about Wordpress.

My other Kindle books

All of my books are available as Kindle books and paperbacks. You can view them all here:

http://amazon.com/author/drandrewwilliams

Here are a few of my more popular books:

Rapid Wordpress Websites

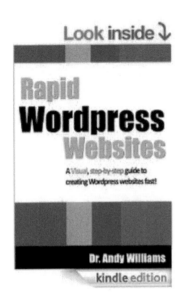

A visual step-by-step guide to building Wordpress websites fast!

Did you ever wish there was a tutorial that would show you just what you needed to know to create your first Wordpress website, without having to wade through stuff you'll never use?

Well this book is that tutorial. It teaches you on a strictly "need-to-know" basis, and will have you building your own website in hours. And I don't leave you stranded either. I created a companion website for readers of this book, with tutorials and help to take your Wordpress skills to the next level, when, and only when, YOU are ready.

What's in this book?

We start at the very beginning by getting good, reliable web hosting and choosing a domain name. I actually walk you through every step, so there will be no confusion.

Once you have your domain, we'll install Wordpress and have a look around the Wordpress Dashboard - think of this as your mission control.

After planning what we want to do, we'll actually build the companion site as we work through the book. We cover the essential settings in Wordpress that you need to know, how to use the editor, the difference between pages and post, categories and tags, etc.

We'll set up custom navigation so your visitors can find their way around your Wordpress site, and carefully use widgets to enhance the design and user experience.

Once the site is built, we'll play around with customizing the look and feel using themes, and I'll point you in the direction of some interesting plugins you might like to look at. These will be covered in more depth on the companion website.

The book will take you from nothing to a complete website in hours, and I'll point out a number of beginner mistakes and things to avoid.

Search Amazon for **B00JGWW86W**

Wordpress for Beginners

Do you want to build a website but scared it's too difficult?

Building a website was once the domain of computer geeks. Not anymore. WordPress makes it possible for anyone to create and run a professional looking website

While WordPress is an amazing tool, the truth is it does have a steep learning curve, even if you have built websites before using different tools. Therefore, the goal of this book is to take anyone, even a complete beginner, and get them building a professional looking website. I'll hold your hand, step-by-step, all the way.

As I was planning this book, I made one decision early on. I wanted to use screenshots of everything so that the reader wasn't left looking for something on their screen that I was describing in text. This book has plenty of screenshots. I haven't counted them all, but it must be close to 300. These images will help you find the things I am talking about. They'll help you check your settings and options against the screenshot of mine. You look, compare, and move on to the next section.

With so many screenshots, you may be concerned that the text might be a little on the skimpy side. No need to worry there. I have described every step of your journey in great detail. In all, this publication has over 35,000 words.

This book will surely cut your learning curve associated with WordPress.

Every chapter of the book ends with a "Tasks to Complete" section. By completing these tasks, you'll not only become proficient at using WordPress, but you'll become confident & enjoy using it too.

Search Amazon for **B009ZVO3H6**

Wordpress SEO

On-Page SEO for your Wordpress Site

Most websites (including blogs) share certain features that can be controlled and used to help (or hinder, especially with Google Panda & Penguin on the loose) with the on-site SEO. These features include things like the page title, headlines, body text, ALT tags and so on. In this respect, most sites can be treated in a similar manner when we consider on-site SEO.

However, different platforms have their own quirks, and WordPress is no exception. Out-of-the-box WordPress doesn't do itself any SEO favours, and can in fact cause you ranking problems, especially with the potentially huge amount of duplicate content it creates. Other problems include static, site-wide sidebars and footers, automatically generated meta tags, page load speeds, SEO issues with Wordpress themes, poorly constructed navigation, badly designed homepages, potential spam from visitors, etc. The list goes on.

This book shows you how to set up an SEO-friendly Wordpress website, highlighting the problems, and working through them with step-by-step instructions on how to fix them.

By the end of this book, your WordPress site should be well optimized, without being 'over-optimized' (which is itself a contributing factor in Google penalties).

Search Amazon for: **B00ECF7OHU**

Search Engine Optimization will Never be the Same Again!

On February 11th, 2011, Google dropped a bombshell on the SEO community when they released the Panda update. Panda was designed to remove low quality content from the search engine results pages. The surprise to many webmasters were some of the big name casualties that got taken out by the update.

On 24th April 2012, Google went in for the kill when they released the Penguin update. Few SEOs that had been in the business for any length of time could believe the carnage that this update caused. If Google's Panda was a 1 on the Richter scale of updates, Penguin was surely a 10. It completely changed the way we needed to think about SEO.

On September 28th 2012, Google released a new algorithm update targeting exact match domains (EMDs). I have updated this book to let you know the consequences of owning EMDs, and added my own advice on choosing domain names. While I have never been a huge fan of exact match domains anyway, many other SEO books and courses teach you to use them. I'll tell you why I think those other courses and books are wrong. The EMD update was sandwiched in between another Panda update (on the 27th September) and another Penguin update (5th October).

Whereas Panda seems to penalize low quality content, Penguin is more concerned about overly aggressive SEO tactics. The stuff that SEOs had been doing for years, not only didn't work anymore, but could now actually cause your site to be penalized and drop out of the rankings. That's right, just about everything you have been taught about Search Engine Optimization in the last 10 years can be thrown out the Window. Google have moved the goal posts.

I have been working in SEO for around 10 years at the time of writing, and have always tried to stay within the guidelines laid down by Google. This has not always been easy because to compete with other sites, it often meant using techniques that Google frowned upon. Now, if you use those techniques, Google is likely to catch up with you and demote your rankings. In this book, I want to share with you the new SEO. **The SEO for 2014 and Beyond.**

An SEO Checklist

A step-by-step plan for fixing SEO problems with your web site

A step-by-step plan for fixing SEO problems with your web site

Pre-Panda and pre-Penguin, Google tolerated certain activities. Post-Panda and post-Penguin, they don't. As a result, they are now enforcing their Webmaster Guidelines which is something that SEOs never really believed Google would do! Essentially, Google have become far less tolerant of activities that they see as rank manipulation.

As webmasters, we have been given a choice. Stick to Google's rules, or lose out on free traffic from the world's biggest search engine.

Those that had abused the rules in the past got a massive shock. Their website(s), which may have been at the top of Google for several years, dropped like a stone. Rankings gone, literally overnight!

To have any chance of recovery, you MUST clean up that site. However, for most people, trying to untangle the SEO mess that was built up over several years is not always easy. Where do you start?

That's why this book was written. It provides a step-by-step plan to fix a broken site. This book contains detailed checklists plus an explanation of why those things are so important.

The checklists in this book are based on the SEO that I use on a daily basis. It's the SEO I teach my students, and it's the SEO that I know works. For those that embrace the recent changes, SEO has actually become easier as we no longer have to battle against other sites whose SEO was done 24/7 by an automated tool or an army of cheap labor. Those sites have largely been removed, and that has leveled the playing field.

If you have a site that lost its rankings, this book gives you a step-by-step plan and checklist to fix problems that are common causes of ranking penalties.

Search Amazon for **B00BXFAULK**

Kindle Publishing

Format, Publish & Promote your books on Kindle

Why Publish on Amazon Kindle?

Kindle publishing has captured the imagination of aspiring writers. Now, more than at any other time in our history, an opportunity is knocking. Getting your books published no longer means sending out hundreds of letters to publishers and agents. It no longer means getting hundreds of rejection letters back. Today, you can write and publish your own books on Amazon Kindle without an agent or publisher.

Is it Really Possible to Make a Good Income as an Indie Author?

The fact that you are reading this book description tells me you are interested in publishing your own material on Kindle. You may have been lured here by promises of quick riches. Well, I have good news and bad. The bad news is that publishing and profiting from Kindle takes work and dedication. Don't just expect to throw up sub-par material and make a killing in sales. You need to produce good stuff to be successful at this. The good news is that you can make a very decent living from writing and publishing on Kindle.

My own success with Kindle Publishing

As I explain at the beginning of this book, I published my first Kindle book in August 2012, yet by December 2012, just 5 months later, I was making what many people consider being a full time income. As part of my own learning experience, I setup a Facebook page in July 2012 to share my Kindle publishing journey (there is a link to the Facebook page inside this book). On that Facebook page, I shared the details of what I did, and problems I needed to overcome. I also shared my growing income reports, and most of all, I offered help to those who asked for it. What I found was a huge and growing audience for this type of education, and ultimately, that's why I wrote this book.

What's in this Book?

This book covers what I have learned on my journey and what has worked for me. I have included sections to answer the questions I myself asked, as well as those questions people asked me. This book is a complete reference manual for successfully formatting, publishing & promoting your books on Amazon Kindle. There is even a section for non-US publishers because there is stuff there you specifically need to know. I see enormous potential in Kindle Publishing, and in 2013 I intend to grow this side of my own business. Kindle publishing has been liberating for me and I am sure it will be for you too.

Search Amazon for **B00BEIX34C**

Self-Publishing on Createspace

Convert & Publish your books on Createspace

Self-publishing your own work is easier than at any time in our history. Amazon's Kindle platform and now Createspace allow us to self-publish our work, with zero costs up front.

Createspace is a fantastic opportunity for writers. You publish your book, and if someone buys it, Createspace print it and send it to the customer. All the author needs to do is wait to be paid. How's that for hands-free and risk-free publishing?

This book takes you step-by-step through my own process for publishing. Topics covered include:

- Basic Text Formatting
- Which Font?
- Links and formatting checks
- Page Numbering in Word
- Adding a new title to Createspace
- Price calculator and deciding on Trim size
- Image DPI requirements
- Paint Shop Pro conversion process
- Common formatting problems
- Book Cover Templates
- Creating the cover with Photoshop Elements
- Creating the cover in Paint Shop Pro
- Submitting the book & cover to Createspace
- Expanded Distribution?

The book also includes links to a number of video tutorials created by the author to help you understand the formatting and submission process.

Search Amazon for **B00HG0GE0C**

Learn CSS with detailed instructions, step-by-step screenshots and video tutorials showing CSS in action on real sites

Most websites and blogs you visit use cascading style sheets (CSS) for everything from fonts selection & formatting, to layout & design. Whether you are building WordPress sites or traditional HTML websites, this book aims to take the complete beginner to a level where they are comfortable digging into the CSS code and making changes to their own site. This book will show you how to make formatting & layout changes to your own projects quickly and easily.

The book covers the following topics:

- Why CSS is important
- Classes, Pseudo Classes, Pseudo Elements & IDs
- The Float property
- Units of Length
- Using DIVs
- Tableless Layouts, including how to create 2-column and 3-column layouts
- The Box Model
- Creating Menus with CSS
- Images & background images

The hands on approach of this book will get YOU building your own Style Sheets from scratch. Also included in this book:

- Over 160 screenshots and 20,000 words detailing ever step you need to take.
- Full source code for all examples shown.
- Video Tutorials.

The video tutorials accompanying this book show you:

- How to investigate the HTML & CSS behind any website.
- How to experiment with your own design in real time, and only make the changes permanent on your site when you are ready.

A basic knowledge of HTML is recommended, although all source code from the book can be downloaded and used as you work through the book.

Search Amazon for **B00AFV44NS**

Migrating to Windows 8.1

For computer users without a touch screen, coming from XP, Vista or Windows 7

Review: "What Microsoft should buy and give away now to drive sales"

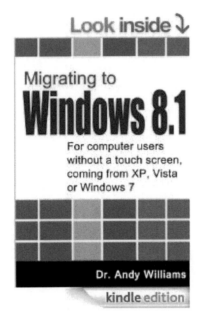

New PCs are coming pre-installed with Windows 8, Microsoft's new incarnation of the popular operating system. The problem is, the PCs it is installed on are not usually equipped with the piece of hardware that Windows 8 revolves around - a touch screen.

Windows 8 is probably the least user-friendly version of the operating system ever released. It's almost like two different operating systems merged together. From the lack of a start menu, to features that only really make sense on a tablet or phone, Windows 8 has a lot of veteran Windows users scratching their heads. If you are one of them, then this book is for you.

After a quick tour of the new user interface, the book digs deeper into the features of Windows 8, showing you what everything does, and more importantly, how to do the things you used to do on older versions of Windows. The comprehensive "How to" section answers a lot of the questions new users have, and there's also a complete keyboard shortcut list for reference.

If you are migrating to Windows 8 from XP, Vista or Windows 7, then this book may just let you keep your hair as you learn how to get the most out of your computer. Who knows, you may even get to like Windows 8.

Search Amazon for **B00CJ8AD9E**

Printed in Germany
by Amazon Distribution
GmbH, Leipzig